Radical Notes 8

Notes From Tomorrow

On Reason, Negation and Certainty

Radical Notes 8

Notes From Tomorrow

On Reason, Negation and Certainty

Werner Bonefeld

NOTES FROM TOMORROW: On Reason, Negation and Certainty
Werner Bonefeld

First Published, 2015

ISBN 978-93-5002-335-8

Published by
AAKAR BOOKS
28 E Pocket IV, Mayur Vihar Phase I, Delhi 110 091
Phone : 011 2279 5505 Telefax : 011 2279 5641
aakarbooks@gmail.com; www.aakarbooks.com

Printed at
Sapra Brothers, Delhi 110 092

A movement in a sense is a struggle over the definition of reality—how reality is constituted. It is this struggle that builds the focus and targets of the movement, informing the praxes towards social transformation. Inherent in this struggle is the act of reclaiming—sense and sensibility, words and meaning...

The word "radical", which in this post-Cold War phase of Global Capitalism or globaloney has been reduced to a general notion characterizing all kinds of extremism and deviance, is one such word that has been time and again reclaimed by the practitioners of social transformation. "Radical" derived from the Latin word, 'radix' meaning 'root' = 'basic' = 'fundamental' is a concept that aptly defines a transformatory practice as an endeavour to reveal and target the essence of what is given to us in appearance. Radicalism in this sense is nothing but fundamental transformation rather than politicking in appearances. Further, and foremost, it is the all-round critique of the status quo and its genealogies, rather than accepting the disciplinary divide/boundaries that the capitalist system perpetuates in order to control labour-power and labour, our efforts and their fruits.

Radical Notes is an endeavour to coordinate the radical voices around the globe, with special focus on South Asia. In our view such focus (which could have been anything) is not just for convenience, given the facilitators' cultural and intellectual comfort, but is also needed to concretise any 'radical' pursuit. In our view South Asia provides us the opportunity to visualize the reproduction of 'global' capitalism and struggle against it in a regional setting. But we must remember such focus is always fluid with the ever-dynamic radical needs of the humanity.

Radical Notes booklets are contributions on social, cultural, political or economic issues from counter-hegemonic perspectives, which need not be confined to any established socialist and communist current of thought (though these approaches are most welcome).

Series Editors
Radical Notes

Contents

Introduction

Certainty

This much is certain. The world as it exists is not true. It is false. It is false because the satisfaction of human needs is merely a sideshow. What counts is the profitable accumulation of some abstract form of wealth, of money that yields more money. What cannot be turned into profit is burned. Failure to make a profit entails great danger. To the vanishing point of death, the life of the dispossessed class of labourers hangs by the success of turning her human effort into a profitable means for another Man. The profitability of her labour is the fundamental condition of achieving and sustaining wage-based employment. For the dispossessed labourer, the alternatives are bleak. The class struggle to sustain access to the means of subsistence and maintain labour conditions is relentless. Yesterday's profitable appropriation of some other person's labour buys another Man today, the buyer for the sake of making another profit so that he may enrich himself, the seller in order to make a living. The relationship between the buyer and seller of labour power amounts in fact to a relationship between the buyer of labour power and the producer of surplus value, the one owning the means of life, the other owning nothing except her labour power, which ties the dispossessed to work as the conditions for waged-based access to the means of subsistence. For the buyer of labour power, the dispossessed labourer is mere human material that transforms the means of life into a profitable investment. For the seller of labour power exploitation is thus more than just forceful extraction of surplus value. It is also the condition of sustained employment and therewith access to the means of life. What really can the seller of redundant labour power trade in its stead—body and body substances: how many for pornography, how many for prostitution, how many for rape, many for kidney sales?

Capitalist wealth entails the pauper in its concept. It recognises the pauper as an entrepreneur of labour power. In a world of entrepreneurs, enterprise counts and the pauper is thus dismissed by political economy as one who did not employ her labour power well. Human significance vanishes in the form of economic quantities that are measured and calculated with winning intent. Man is the existing untruth in her own social world—at worst, she figures as a metaphysical distraction in the game of numbers. At best, she is recognised as the human material of economic quantities—a factor of production, a mere resource, a means for profit. Some say, she needs to be paid more and work in better conditions. This is undoubtedly the case. Still its truth is a moment of the false. As an existing untruth, society as an economic subject manifests the topsy-turvy world of price and profit in the demand for a just treatment of the mistreated—the nimble fingers deserve a better deal, a new deal to achieve better paid nimble fingers!.

Time is money and money makes the world go round, and money is money only as more money. In this dazzling world, Man is little more than a time's carcass. Life-time is labour time. The class tied to work struggles for life-time on the condition that its labour time is competitive on a world market scale, making a profit for her employer as the condition of preventing the redundancy of her labour power maintaining employment. Failure to achieve this competitive edge over her labouring brothers and sisters reduces this struggle for lifetime to a desperate scramble to make ends meet. On the pain of ruin, the existing relations of wealth demand from the Many that they become self-responsible entrepreneurs of their labour power, always eager and ready to adjust to the movement of the economic forces, whatever it takes in order to make ends meet.

Society as the subject of economic forces moves in mysterious ways—here Man manifests itself as the object of the movement of economic things. The real social subject is the economic thing. Political economy captures this when it says that society as economic subject is regulated by the invisible hand. The invisible is beyond human control. In its secular manifestation the invisible appears in the form of great economic success for the few or bankruptcy, profitability or insolvency, wage-based access to subsistence or redundancy of labour power. Without warning and at the blink of an eye, the invisible force of capitalist wealth, the force of economic things, cuts off the supply of the means of subsistence to a whole class of individuals, measured by the rates of unemployment and poverty. The dogma of the false society is that there is no alternative to it, that is, its falsehood is righteous. It celebrates the increase in economic quantities as the measure of certain economic success and declares that the uncertainty of human existence is a price well worth paying for the achievement of economic progress—in this progress of money as more money for its own sake, human material is accumulated on the pyramids of abstract wealth.

A critical social theory that explores the meaning of the economic forces and the categories of price and profit is often either rejected as a form of economic reductionism that stands accused of reducing refined social values to economic calculation, or belittled for its alleged analytical blindness that condemns it to perceive of society as an economic derivative. These views contain elements of false truth. The economy really does not have an independent existence. In its entirety capitalist economy is a perverted form of human social relations. That is, the idea of a social theory beyond the critique of political economy is innately optimistic about the prospects of society. Having freed itself from the fateful economic forces, which movements establish the access to the means of subsistence, sociology becomes a discipline without society. It does not talk about the devil and looks on the bright side. It thus recognises the poverty of nations, if indeed its analytical gaze turns upon it at all, as a miserable market situation, which resolution demands a hegemonic shift in the balance of the contesting social forces to bring in a government that governs for the dispossessed producers of surplus value. Sociology without a concept of society does not ask about the social conditions of misery. The experience of misery is alien to it. Misery revolts.

Hegemony is not a critical concept. Its grasp of society is entirely traditional in that it views society as nothing more than a manifestation of the balance of class forces. This conception of the social forces is purely instrumental. It rejects the hegemony of the capitalist interests, demands the hegemony of the working class, argues for class struggle as the means at shifting the balance of class forces in favour of the working class, and leaves the category of 'capital' entirely untouched by thought. What really does it mean to say that the working class has to become hegemonic in capitalism? Is capital really nothing more than some economic means that is corrupted by the capitalist interests? In its practical dimension, the struggle for hegemony amounts to 'ticket thinking'. Such thinking is 'one-dimensional'. It argues in the interests of the dispossessed traders in labourer power with a claim to power. That is, instead of stopping to make capitalism, it demands to govern for the sake of a capitalism that works for the workers. The last century was filled with dogmas that have cost us time, suffering, and much injustice. It rejected the critique of class society by speaking out for the working class. The critical judgement according to which the being of the productive labourer is a great misfortune was thus turned on its head, leading to the dogma of the productive labourer is an ontological privilege. It thus embraced the mad utopia of a rationalised labour economy as the solution to the capitalist question.

The critical concept is governmentality. Society as the economic subject of money that begets more money is hostile to the needs of the social individuals and yet, it is their work. Neither the capitalist nor the banker, nor indeed the worker can extricate themselves from the reality in which they live and which asserts itself not only over them but also through them, and by means of them. Society as an economic subject prevails through the individuals. Money does not only make the world go round; its possession establishes the connection to the means of life. The struggle for life is a struggle for money—it governs the mentality of bourgeois society and establishes the forces of coined freedom. What a misery! In the face of great social wealth, the dispossessed sellers of labour power struggle for fleeting amounts of money to sustain themselves from one day to the next as the readily available human material for capitalist wealth. Class and struggle are categories of the false society. Its progress has to come to a stop—but how?

Only a reified consciousness can declare that it is in possession of the requisite knowledge, political capacity, and technical expertise not only for resolving capitalist crises but, also, to do so in the interests of the class right to work. Its world-view describes capitalist economy as an irrationally organised economy of labour, and proposes socialism as a rationally organised economy of labour by means of conscious planning by public authority, then as now. The anti-capitalism of central economic planning is entirely abstract in its critique of the capitalistically organised mode of social reproduction. For the sake of progress, it demands a rationalised labour economy. 'Abstract negativity' barks in perpetuity and without bite. Instead, it sniffs out the miserable world, from the outside as it were, and puts itself forward as having the capacity, ability, insight, and means for resolving the crisis of capitalist economy 'for the workers'. Abstract negativity describes the theology of anti-capitalism. Theologically conceived, anti-capitalism is devoid of Now-Time. Instead, it views the present as transition towards its own progressive future, promising deliverance from misery amidst 'a pile of debris' that 'grows skyward' (Benjamin 1999: 249).

Uncertainty and Negation

It is easy to say what is wrong with capitalism. It is much more difficult to decide what therefore needs to be done. The biggest danger of a critique of capitalism is that it itself becomes reified. While every individual is 'ruled by economic abstractions', the owners of great wealth experience this rule as a source of great enrichment and power. In this context the 'rulers' are safe for as long as the 'ruled' struggle under the spell of the capitalist world, in which, say, the cause of financial crisis, economic downturn, and conditions of austerity are attributed to the greedy behaviour of identifiable individuals. A spellbound critique of capitalism demands more of this and less of that. It apportions blame and proclaims to know 'how to set things right'. Rather than capital, it is, say, the profit-making consciousness of the capitalist and the greed of the speculator that is criticised, rejected, and condemned. That is, the critique of the capitalist manifests itself as a demand for a better capitalism, one that works in the interests of the 'workers'. Marx's critique of Proudhon focused on this simple point. Proudhon substituted the critique of the capitalism for a critique of the capitalist, seeking to free capital from the capitalist so as to utilise the power of capital for the benefit of a well-ordered society, investing in society.

The critique of the capitalist leaves the category of capital not only entirely untouched, it also elevates 'capital' as a thing beyond critique. Capital thus appears to be no more than an economic mechanism that can be made to work for this class interest or that class interest—in the end, it is the balance of the class forces that decide for which interest capital functions. The idea that slave society should work in the interests of the slaves is as absurd as the demand that capital society should be made to work in the interests of the class tied to work.

The critique of the capitalist does not touch the category of capital by thought. Instead, it identifies the guilty party, condemns it, and demands state action to sort things out and set things right. It thus attributes miserable social conditions to the conscious activity of some identifiable individuals, who no longer appear as the personification of economic categories but, rather, as the personalised subject of misery. This personalisation of the economic categories entails a number of differentiations, most importantly between the productive or indeed creative capitalist as a 'producer' of 'real' wealth employing a hard-working and creative people, and the financial or indeed parasitic capitalist who makes his fortune by speculating in money to the detriment of industry and workers. Here the distinction between a concrete labour that produces things for use, on the one hand, and exchange value that manifests itself in exchange in the form of money, on the other, appears in the forms of distinct personalities—pitting the creative industrialist against the parasitic banker-cum-speculator. There emerges, then, the idea of a capitalism that is corrupted by the financial interests. Finance turns capitalism into a casino that turns the fortune wheel of the world at the expense of national industry, national wealth, national workers, and national harmony. That is, a definite form of society manifests itself in the form of a movement of coins and then, under the spell this coined movement, rebels against the personifications of a world governed by coins. The personalised critique of capital identifies the 'wrongdoer' of the wronged society and calls him a merchant of greed. For the sake of employment and industry, something needs to be done. Something can be done! The personalised critique of capitalist social relations is open to abuse from the outset. It thinks akin to a register of blame, and condemns the identified party as a power that hides behind the economic phenomena, sucking the living life out of the national community of hard-working people. This identification of the subject of misery leads to the condemnation of the world market society of capital as a network of money and power that imposes itself with destructive force on a national people who appear thus as victims of the cosmopolitan peddlers (see Bonefeld, 2014).

The critique of financial imperialism entails the idea of anti-imperialism as a progressive, liberating force. The reverse of anti-imperialism is national liberation, by which the dominated national communities defend their identity in opposition to the disintegrating forces of financial globalisation and imperial power. The idea of the nation as a subject of liberation is as irrational as the belief in a national destiny and a national homogeneity of purposes, from the national industry via the national interest to the national history. The idea of the nation as the foundation of being and becoming recognises the term 'cosmopolitanism' as a term of abuse. In its stead, it puts its faith in the imagined nation as some naturally rooted and active thing, which it idolises as the 'spirit of the people'. If indeed it is permissible at all to speak about the national spirit of the people, it is a national spirit not by nature, but by history. By reducing history to nature or by reading nature into history, the struggle for national liberation becomes delusional inasmuch as a people are forced to act as if they really are natural forces that have a national history. This critique is entirely regressive. In opposition to the world of capital, it proclaims for the liberation of some presumed oppressed national nature, pitting the pseudo concreteness of the wronged nation against the perceived enemy of the national harmony of interests.

Postscript

The coined freedom that characterises the progress of capitalist society is marked by the terror of dispossession. In the face of immense wealth, the struggle for access to crude material things, the means of life, is constant. This struggle does not follow some abstract idea. It is an experienced struggle in which life becomes truly restless: the multitudinous struggle for subsistence entails the struggle for the means of life. This struggle is savage, as is its democracy. In distinction to the coined freedom of bourgeoisie society, in which labour power is traded for the sake of making a profit for its buyer and in which the political state is the concentrated force of depoliticised exchange relations between the buyers and sellers of labour power, the struggle for the means of life politicises society and thus negates the distinction between state and society. It establishes however fleetingly the direct democracy of the free and equal. Its reality is its own uncertainty. Uncertainty does not await its genesis. It is born in dispossession and struggle and prevails through the struggle to make ends meet—it is a struggle for life. Its reality is savage. Whether the savage struggle for the means of life turns concrete in the changing forms of repression as resistance to repression or whether it turns concrete in forms of repression, is a matter of experienced history. There is as much experience of history as there is struggle to stop the progress of the 'muck of ages and found society anew' (Marx and Engels 1956). Communism is the name of this negation.

Structure

The three chapters that follow explore the themes of the Introduction—*Anti-Globalisation versus Anti-Capitalism—The Dangers of Nationalism, Racism and Anti-Semitism* rejects the maddening content of a critique of capitalism that personalises nature and blames identifiable individuals for the social human misery that is fundamental for the progress of capitalism. *History and Human Emancipation: Struggle, Uncertainty, and Openness* argues against the idea of history as an unfolding force. It argues that history is made and that it therefore takes no site. *Notes on Fetishism, History and Uncertainty: Beyond the Critique of Austerity* takes this argument further, arguing that history has been the history of the victors of history. The time for this history has to come to an end is now, a point which the chapters explore with reference to Benjamin's Now-Time. The concluding chapter *On the Question of Alternatives* challenges the anti-austerity left. It argues that communism is the alternative to capitalism.

REFERENCES

Bonefeld, Werner. *Critical Theory and the Critique of Political Economy* (New York 2014).

Benjamin, Walter. 'Theses on the Philosophy of History', in *Illuminations*, edited and introduced by Hanna Arendt (London 1999).

Marx, Karl and Engels, Friederich. *The German Ideology, Collected Works*, Vol. 5 (London 1976).

1

Anti-Globalisation versus Anti-Capitalism

The Dangers of Nationalism, Racism and Anti-Semitism

Preface

During the last decade we have seen the deep recession of the early 1990s, the European currency crises of 1992 and 1993, the plunge of the Mexican peso in December 1994 which rocked financial markets around the world, the Asian crisis of 1997, the Russian crisis of 1998, the Brazilian crisis of 1999, and the Argentinean crisis of 2001. Japan teeters on the edge of depression and then there is the speculative bubble in the New York Stock Exchange and the dramatic global slowdown. There is hardly a day without warnings about the immanent burst of the bubble and a worldwide depression. The nightmare of a full-scale world economic crisis, world war and unfettered barbarism cannot easily be excluded as a real possibility. 'We know how rapidly an epoch of global prosperity, underpinning prospects of world peace and international harmony, can become an epoch of global confrontation, culminating in war. If such a prospect seems unlikely now, it seemed equally unlikely a century ago' (Clarke, 2001, p. 91) and it seems more likely today than only yesterday. How many wars have been fought since the end of the cold war and how many will follow in the years to come? And then there is terrorism. The events of September 11 demonstrated with brutal force the impotence of sense, significance, and thus reason and ultimately truth. The denial of human quality and difference was absolute—not even their corpses survived. And the response? It confirmed that state terrorism and terrorism are two sides of the same coin. Between them, nothing is allowed to survive.

Many critics of globalisation urge the creation of new forms of political regulation at the national and international level to humanise global capital, containing its 'neo-liberal' self-destructive force in favour of the common good. What, however, is the common good in a capitalistically constituted form of social reproduction? The 'good' appears to be the creation of wealth that capital is able to achieve for all, if it is made accountable to liberal-democratic forms of regulation. Yet, does the humanisation of inhuman conditions not presuppose these same conditions as eternal? Regardless of its historically changing forms (Agnoli, 1997, Clarke, 1992), the function of the capitalist state has always been to secure the common good of a capitalistically organised form of social reproduction: capitalist accumulation (cf. Agnoli, 2002).

The great scandal of global capital is that it is choking itself up on the pyramids of accumulated abstract wealth. Yet, when looking at social conditions, when listening to the ever more urgent demand for greater labour flexibility, it seems as if the global crisis is really just a consequence of a scarcity of capital. This is indeed the conclusion one would have to reach when one looks at Africa's misery, when one sees the thousands and thousands of children living in poverty, not just in Africa, not just in Latin America and Asia, not just in those areas of the world deemed inessential by global capital but also in the centres of globalisation, in Western Europe and the USA. Yet, the dramatic increase in poverty and misery across the globe is not caused by conditions of economic scarcity. There is too much capital, too many commodities that can not be sold for profit, too many workers are 'overexploited', on the one hand, and, on the other, too many workers are not even exploitable. Over the last two decades, profits have risen and so too has unemployment. Labour productivity has increased dramatically and poverty has increased, wages have stagnated, and conditions deteriorated. Marx focused this 'constellation' well when he argued that '[S]ociety suddenly finds itself put back into a state of momentary barbarism; it appears as if famine, a universal war of devastation had cut off the supply of every means of subsistence; industry and commerce seem to be destroyed; and why? Because there is too much civilisation, too much means of subsistence; too much industry, too much commerce. The productive forces at the disposal of society no longer tend to further the development of the conditions of bourgeois property; on the contrary, they have become too powerful for these conditions, by which they are fettered, and as soon as they overcome these fetters, they bring disorder into the whole of bourgeois society, endanger the existence of bourgeois property. The conditions of bourgeois society are too narrow to comprise the wealth created by them. And how does bourgeois society get over these crises? On the one hand by enforced destruction of a mass of productive forces; on the other, by the conquest of new markets, and by the more thorough exploitation of the old ones' (Marx and Engels, 1996, pp. 18–19).

The contemporary conditions of poverty, misery, hopelessness, and hunger are not just an appearance of the contradictions of capitalist social reproduction on a global scale. They are also sharp reminders of a conception of progress that entailed barbarism from its inception.[1] Critics argue, rightly, that if unchecked, globalisation will lead to barbarism. However, barbarism has already been. In relation to an earlier resolution to global crisis, Adorno's (1990) insight demands serious consideration: Auschwitz, he argued, not only confirmed the violence of the bourgeois relations of abstract equality and abstract identity. It also confirmed the bourgeois exchange relations of pure identity as death. It is, however, the case that the horror of Auschwitz persists as a barbaric solution to crisis for as long as those social relations exist that made Auschwitz possible (Adorno, 1969, p. 85).

Negt (2001) is surely right when he charges many left critics of globalisation for their failure to offer any views on how the accumulated wealth can be used to liberate millions and millions of people, not only in the 'developing' societies but in the centres of wealth too, from conditions of misery, poverty and starvation; and on how socially necessary labour can be organised to meet human needs. Critics urge the creation of new forms of political regulation at the national and international level to contain capital's 'neoliberal' self-destructive force in favour of the common good. In opposition to global institutions like the WTO which are seen to affirm neoliberal values and institutionalise an unfair system of trade, critics urge the renewal of democratic controls of capital so as to regulate trade more fairly and limit the power of global finance and global financial institutions that keep so-called developing nations in debt and force them further into debt. Others call for the de-linking of 'developing' countries from the world market to secure national economic development. Globalisation is seen here as a form of American imperialism and global institutions, like the IMF, are seen as agencies of US imperial power. National self-determination is seen as a socialist opposition to imperialist globalisation. What, however, is anti-capitalistic in anti-capitalism when it seeks to regulate capital without touching the relations of exploitation, when it poses the national state as the sovereign power that places controls on capital to secure the common national good? What is the common national good? The function and role of the national state is to achieve homogeneity of national conditions. In its liberal conception, this means the equality of all before the law. In its Leninist conception, it means the equality of labour. In its nationalist version it means equality as a nation, as a Volk. In its essence, the nationalist conception of equality in terms of Volk entails the projection of a classless 'national community' whose existence is seen to be threatened by the 'external enemy within'.

The anti-globalisation movement of the political Left originated, in Europe at least, against the new anti-immigration populist right led by, for example, Le Pen in France, Haider in Austria, and also Hanson in Australia. The populist right poses national identity and communality as a response to the perceived threats of globalisation. The common feeling of these nationalist forces was well focused by Mahathir Mohamad, the

Prime Minister of Malaysia. His assessment of Malaysia's financial collapse in 1997 is symptomatic: 'I say openly, these people are racists. They are not happy to see us prosper. They say we grow too fast, they plan to make us poor. We are not making enemies with other people but others are making enemies with us'.[2] Leaving aside the discrimination of particularly Malaysian citizens of Chinese background aside, what is meant by 'we' and who are the racialised 'they'?

In its structure, the conception of 'speculators' as the external enemy bent on destroying relations of national economy harmony, belongs to modern anti-Semitism. It summons the idea of finance and speculators as merchants of greed and, counterposed to this, espouses the idea of a national community. In the nationalist conception of equality, the 'folk is "subject to blood", it arises from the "soil", it furnishes the homeland with indestructible force and permanence, it is united by characteristics of "race", the preservation of whose purity is the condition of the folk's "health" (Marcuse, 1988, p. 23). Nationalism offers a barbaric solution to globalisation. The evocation of the external enemy serves to displace the focus from the inherent antagonism of capitalism and projects the racialist figure of an external intruder as the cause of national disharmony and misfortune. The traditional figure of this ideological projection is the 'Jew'.

The nerve-centre of barbarism is a fetishistic critique of global relations that projects a class-ridden society as a national community, subsuming, through arson and murder, class relations into the abstract identity of national sameness—the national 'we'. National wealth and autonomy is seen to be undermined by external forces that disrupt the integrity of national economies. Thus 'national disharmony' is merely imported from the outside. The nationalist critique of global capital, then, favours the strong and capable state to restore the cohesion, integrity, and wealth creating potentials of its national economy against threats to stability from the outside. Historically, the restoration of 'national harmony' developed through war and the transformation of economies into war economies. This transformation depends on the creation of the national 'we' and thus on the identification and persecution of the 'external' enemy within. This machination is inherently racist and can easily tip over into anti-Semitism. Racism stands for a barbaric conception of 'equality' and, as this essay argues, anti-Semitism is the objective ideology of barbarism that makes anti-capitalism directly useful for capitalism. It amounts to a fetishistic critique of bourgeois notions of equality in favour of an abstract national identity, of *Volk*.

Racism and anti-Semitism are different-in-unity. All forms of racism project the Other as a disintegrating power, allegedly undermining the integration of the much-praised one-national boat that ostensibly is threatened by globalisation. Racism projects the power of the Other as a 'sub-human' (*Untermenschen*) power. This 'power' is in contrast to anti-Semitism, perceived as a rooted power. That is, the projected Other is seen to be rooted either nationally (Turks should live in Turkey, not in Germany; black Americans come from Africa and are Africans) or should accept their position of inferiority as 'sub-humans' within 'nations' without question. Racism regulates the Other through institutional racism, forced return to 'their homeland', segregation, racial profiling, as well as arson and murder. Racism transposes feudal relations of social hierarchy, position and privilege on to bourgeois society, modernising, as it were, the relations between master and slave as relations of an 'organic' society sustaining the abstract exchange relations of capital through the racist differentiation of the dependent masses, and that is, the institutional regulation of racialised underclass.

Anti-Semitism, in contrast, projects the Other as rootless. For the anti-Semite, the Jew comes from nowhere. Lyotard (1993, p. 159) summarises this projection well. 'The Jews are not a nation. They do not speak a language of their own. They have no roots in a nature...They claim to have their roots in a book'. The anti-Semite does not project the Jew as sub-human. Instead, theirs is the power of an immensely powerful, intangible, international conspiracy (cf. Postone, 1986). Their power cannot be defined concretely. 'Anti-Semitism is the rumour about Jews' (Adorno, 1951, p. 141). The Jew is seen as the one who stands behind phenomena. Racism's projection of the Other as a real or potential slave contrasts with anti-Semitism's projection of the Jew as evil personified. This Other can thus not be regulated, neither politically nor economically. It has to be, as the anti-Semites have it, destroyed, that is, exterminated.

Introduction

In the Preface to his *Philosophy of Right,* Hegel argued that those who render abstractions effective in social life are engaged in the destruction of social reality. Human values such as honesty, sincerity, tolerance, and especially dignity have no price and cannot be quantified, neither sold nor bought. These values connote individual human distinctiveness, difference, sense and significance, that is, Man (*Mensch*) in possession of himself as a subject. Yet, we are used to think in terms of abstractions, such as capital, the market, the state, the nation, etc. These, following Sohn-Rhetel's (1970) terminology, are really existing abstractions. The purpose of Marx's critique of fetishism was to demystify their ostensibly objective force and to show that their apparent independence is an objective delusion. He argued that their objective force has a real existence as forms of social relations, that is, as forms constituted and reproduced through human social practice. Their objective delusion is fostered by the capitalist exchange relations themselves. They suggest that rationally acting subjects meet on the market to realise their rational interests, whereas in fact they act as executives of abstract social laws which they themselves have generated historically and reproduce through their rational behaviour and over which they have no control (Reichelt, 2002, p. 143).

In the false totality of bourgeois society it takes courage to demystify abstractions. Dignity has no price. It can however be destroyed when critical-practical judgment is suspended through the identification of really existing humans as mere personifications of abstractions. There is only one human standard which, though unchangeable and indivisible, can be lost—through the imposition of abstract identity (cf. Adorno, 1990). Thinking in terms of abstractions is all-pervasive. This is especially relevant in relation to Israel. Israel is rightly condemned for its policy towards the Palestinians. This condemnation, however, all too easily takes anti-Semitic forms as the difference between really existing individuals and their coercive integration in the form of the state is purged. The mounting scale and sheer extent of the anti-Semitic tidal wave especially in the Middle East has blurred any distinction between the rightful critique of Israeli nationalism and concrete persons, including their class divided mode of existence. Just as the management of the Israeli class conflict through the militarisation of its policy towards the Palestinians, Islamist struggle for national self-determination is commandeered by leaders to achieve, not the emancipation of a people, but their own political emancipation in the form of the national state. Many on the left tend to dismiss rampant Islamist anti-Semitism as a mere epiphenomenona of justified anger at Israel and US imperialism. Susan George's (quoted in Callinicos, 2003) description of al Qaeda as fascist fundamentalists drew a rebuke from Callinicos who argued that the Muslim concept *ummah* contrasts to the fascist doctrine of blood and soil because it is a transnational one. Al Qaeda, he rightly points out, incorporates activists from many different national backgrounds. He forgets that blood and soil included the 'transnational doctrine' and practice of Lebensraum and that the composition of the SS incorporated many different national backgrounds, including British subjects. Nevertheless, Callinicos is right: historical analogies offer little in terms of analysis and explanation. Yet, if the understanding of fascism is restricted to the experience of European fascist regimes, then fascism has no longer to be feared. Conditions change. It is, however, not the past but the present that demonstrates truth and that is, the potential of fascism's return has to be ascertained against the background of contemporary class struggles and conditions. Herein lies the challenge of George's characterisation. Ideologically, fascist ideology belongs to the far right. However, for fascism to become effective, it has to become an extremism of the political centre. The contemporary transformation of the bourgeois state into a market-liberal security state poses this fascist potential.

Islamic fundamentalism can itself be seen as a reaction

against the 'heavy artillery' of global capital to create a world after its own image. Against this, Islamic fundamentalism espouses the quest for authenticity, seeking to preserve through the purification of imagined ancestral conditions and traditions existing social structures. The fight against 'westoxication', as Khomeini called the ideas of liberalism, democracy and socialism, indicates that Islamic anti-Semitism is unlikely to be assuaged by an Israeli-Palestinian settlement. It is more likely to be inflamed. At base, it is the depiction of Israel as an imperialist bridgehead of 'Jewish' capitalist counterinsurgency that fuels the hatred of Israel as a 'Jewish' state. What one may ask is a Jewish state? The attribute might refer to a concrete human being, for example Sharon or Marx, Einstein or Emma Goldman, or it might summon those projected abstract qualities that anti-Semitism calls its own; this deadly displacement from the focus on class antagonism to the racialist other.

In Marx's *Jewish Question* and the writings of the Frankfurt School, the category 'Jew' stands for a social metaphor. In contrast, however, to the affirmative categorisation 'Jew', it was a critical category that challenged 'categorisation'. That is, the meaning and significance of the 'Jewish Question' was approached through the lens of the critique of the fetishism of the commodity form. Expanding on Marx's critical question, 'why does this content [human social relations] assume that form [the form of capital]' (cf. Marx, 1962, p. 95), the Jewish question as a critical category asks why does the bourgeois critique of capitalism assume the form of anti-Semitism? In contrast, the affirmative use of the category 'Jew' rationalises anti-Semitism as a manifestation of the hatred of capitalism, and through its rationalisation, is complicit in the perversion of anti-capitalism that is directly useful for capitalism itself.

The essay focuses on that form of anti-Semitism that found its raison d'être in Auschwitz. Such an examination sheds light on the contemporary connection between globalisation and nationalist anti-globalisation. The essay argues that anti-Semitism is directly related with 'modernity's' attempt at reconciling its constituting contradiction, which is the class antagonism between capital and labour. Horkheimer's (1988,

p. 9) dictum that whoever wants to talk about Fascism but not about capitalism should shut up, puts this contention into sharp focus and raises, against the background of the contemporary militarisation of foreign and domestic policies, the issue of its contemporary significance. The conclusion returns to the wider discussion on anti-globalisation and offers some suggestions.

In what follows, I have freely borrowed from Horkheimer and Adorno (1989) and Postone (1986). In their *Dialectic of the Enlightenment*, Horkheimer and Adorno emphasise that Enlightenment's 'reason' obtains fundamentally as 'instrumental reason' or 'instrumental rationality'. The determination of 'reason' as reason being denied in the form of 'instrumental reason' entails that instrumental reason is reason's false friend and that, as such a friend, it negates reason's promise to destroy all relations where humanity exists as a resource. Horkheimer and Adorno build on discussion of anti-Semitism as a form of hatred that identifies Jews as the representatives of the sphere of capital circulation, especially in its most elementary form of 'M...M'', and argue that anti-Semitism projects Jews as personifications of global capital, leading to the murderous demand that the liberation from capital amounts to the liberation from Jews. Postone deepens this insight arguing that anti-Semitism amounts to a fetish critique of capital and thus to a critique on the basis of capital. Anti-Semitism is a constituted form of the capital fetish: it amounts to a perverted, bourgeois form of anti-capitalism that is directly useful for capitalism. The critique of anti-Semitism amounts thus to a critique of those forms of anti-capitalism that do not oppose, but rather derive their rationale from constituted capitalist forms (see Marx, 1964).

Reason, Anti-Semitism and Equality

Anti-Semitism does not 'need' Jews. The category 'Jew' has powers attributed to it that cannot be defined concretely. It is an abstraction that excludes nobody. Anyone can be considered a Jew. The concept 'Jew' knows no individuality, cannot be a man or a woman, and cannot be seen as a worker or beggar; the word 'Jew' relates to a non-person, an abstraction. 'The Jew is one whom other men consider a Jew' (Sartre, 1976, p. 69). For anti-Semitism to rage, the existence of 'Jews' is neither incidental nor required. 'Anti-Semitism tends to occur only as part of an interchangeable programme', the basis of which is the 'universal reduction of all specific energy to the one, same abstract form of labour, from the battlefield to the studio' (Horkheimer and Adorno, 1989, p. 207). Thus, anti-Semitism belongs to a social world in which sense and significance are sacrificed in favour of compliance with the norms and rules of a political and economic reality that poses sameness, ritualised repetition, and objectless subjectivity as Man's only permitted mode of existence. Difference, and therewith the elevation of human dignity to a purpose of social existence, beyond and above the ritualised mentality of empty and idle thought stands rejected. The mere existence of difference, a difference that signals happiness beyond a life of rationalised production and its expansion into every area of social life fosters the blind resentment and anger that anti-Semitism focuses and exploits but does not itself produce (cf. ibid., pp. 207-08).

Anti-Semitism differentiates between 'society' and 'national community'. 'Society' is identified as 'Jewish'; whereas community is modelled as a counter-world to society. Community is seen to be constituted by nature and 'nature' is seen to be at risk because of 'evil' abstract social forces. The attributes given by the anti-Semite to Jews include mobility, intangibility, rootlessness and conspiracy against the values and cohesion of an 'ancestral', that is, original community. The presumed 'well-being' of this community is seen to be at the mercy of evil powers: intellectual thought, abstract rules and laws, and the disintegrating forces of communism and finance capital. Both, communism and finance capital are seen as uprooting powers and as entities of reason, and both are seen as the property of the rootless intelligence of 'Jews', an intelligence based on reason and critical judgment.[3] Reason stands rejected because of its infectious desire to leave behind relations of domination and exploitation. Reason is the weapon of critique. It challenges conditions where Man is degraded to a mere resource that stands to attention clicking his heels to receive the commands of those who demand the transformation of the world into one huge factory of commandeered labour. For the anti-Semite independence of thought and the ability to think freely without fear, is abhorrent. It detests the idea that *'Man is the highest being for Man'* [*Mensch*] (Marx, 1975, p. 182). Instead, it seeks deliverance through murder. It the anti-Semites that produce the 'Jew', and the anti-Semites' portrayal of the Jew as evil personified is in fact their own self-portrait.

Anti-Semitism has always been based on an urge, which its instigators held against the Social Democrats: the urge for equality. Social Democracy sees equality as emanating from the project of the Enlightenment. It urges equality to achieve a just and fair society. This demand focuses on citizenship rights for all and on the sphere of distribution where equality of opportunity is seen as a civil good compensating for the absence of humanity at the point of production. Anti-Semitism urges a different sort of equality. It derives equality from membership in a national community. This equality is defined by the mythical 'property' of land and soil based on the bond of blood. Blood and soil are configured as the mythical bond of a national community. The fetish of blood and soil is itself rooted in the capital fetish where the concrete in the form of use value obtains only in and through the abstract in the form of exchange value. Anti-Semitism construes blood, soil, and also machinery as concrete counter-principles of the abstract. The abstract is personified in the category Jew. The anti-Semitic revolt, then, against the abstract amounts to a conformist rebellion in favour of the fascist extension of the capitalist factory discipline to society at large. For the apologists of market liberalism, the reference to the invisible hand operates like an explanatory refuge. It explains everything with reference to the Invisible. 'Starvation is God's way of punishing those who have too little faith in capitalism' (Rockefeller Sr., quoted in Marable, 1991, p. 147). For the anti-Semites, however, the power of the invisible can be explained—the Jew is its personification and biologised existence. It transforms anti-capitalist anger about social injustice into a conformist rebellion against the projected personification of capitalism.

The nationalist conception of equality defines 'society' as

the Other—a parasite whose objective is deemed to oppress, undermine and pervert the 'natural community' through the 'disintegrating' force of the abstract and intangible values of bourgeois civilisation. The category 'Jew' is seen to personify abstract thought and abstract equality, including its incarnation, money. The Volksgenosse, then, is seen as somebody who resists 'Jewish' abstract values and instead upholds some sort of natural equality. Their 'equality' as Jews obtains as a construct to which all those belong who deviate from the conception of the *Volksgenosse*, that is, mythical concrete matter. The myth of the Jew is confronted with the myth of the original possession of soil, elevating nationalism's 'regressive equality' (Adorno, 1951, p. 56) to a liberating action. The *Volkgenosse* sees himself as a son of nature and thus as a natural being. He sees his natural destiny in the liberation of the national community from allegedly rootless, abstract values, demanding their naturalisation so that everything is returned to 'nature'. In short, the *Volksgenosse* portrays himself as rooted in blood and ancestral tradition to defend his own faith in the immorality of madness through the collective approval of anger. This anger is directed towards civilisation's supposed victory over nature, a victory that is seen as condemning the *Volksgenosse* to sweat, toil and physical effort, whereas the Other is seen to live a life as banker and speculator. This the *Volksgenosse* aspires for himself with murder becoming the climax of his aspiration. The *Volksgenosse* speculates in death and banks the extracted gold teeth.

For the *Volksgenossen*, the Jews 'are the scapegoats not only for individual manoeuvres and machinations but in a broader sense, inasmuch as the economic injustice of the whole class is attributed to them' (Horkheimer and Adorno, 1989, p. 174). Pogroms are not only conceived as a liberating action but, also, as a moral obligation: anti-Semitism calls for a 'just' revenge on the part of the 'victimised' national community against the powers of 'rootless' society. 'Community' is seen to be both victimised and 'strong'. Strength is derived from the biological conception of the national community: blood constituted possession and tradition. This biologisation of community finds legitimation for murder in the biologisation of the 'action': biology is conceived as a destiny. From this follows the demand to overturn and break society's hold on community in order for the latter to reassert its assumed authenticity and purity.

Reason that escorted the primitive accumulation of capital with the promise of human dignity, appears transformed into the idle occupation of killing for the sake of killing. Kant's notion that reason was to lead mankind to maturity formulated reason's claim to think beyond itself in order to find deliverance in significance and meaning, in humanity. This is reason's revolutionary imperative. However, reason is not one-sided; it has a darker side, as de Sade showed. This darker side subsists as instrumental rationality, a joyless rationality interested only in calculability be it in terms of an all pervasive market rationality or fordist production processes. Instrumental rationality does not know human values. Everything and everybody is just a tool, a utility, in the forward march of accumulation for accumulation's sake. For instrumental rationality, human values are a scandal for they inhibit the full utilisation of technical efficacy and humanity is merely conceived as an irritating factor of production, a living resource that has to be integrated into the well-oiled systems of economic production and political machines. Reason's claim to lead the exodus to a better world and the resourceful rationality of instrumental reason are two halves of the same walnut: Revolution and its containment in the name of revolution itself. 'The thought of happiness without power is unbearable because it would then be true happiness' (ibid., p. 172). Instrumental reason allows merely technological revolutions and is interested merely in the corrosion of character—Men with no qualities, humans of standardised and yet flexible issue, always prepared to be called upon to function as resourceful tools for profitable calculations, whatever the 'product'. All that instrumental rationality wishes for itself is how best to achieve the optimum result, how best to increase efficiency be it in terms of produced cars or gassed corpses. It is interested only in quantifiable results regardless of content. The efficient organisation and the cold, dispassionate execution of the deed— the cruelty of silence in the house of the hangman —is mirrored by its disregard for individuality: corpses all look the same when counting the results and they are equal to each other; and nothing distinguishes a number from a number except the difference in quantity—the measure of success. The mere existence of happiness is a provocation. Judgment is suspended. Everybody is numbered and assessed for use.

Anti-Semitism's stigmatisation of reason and money as evil not only mythologises reason and money as forces that come, like their projected personifications, the Jew, from nowhere. It also produces the legend that those with a 'home', 'tradition', 'roots' and 'soil' are mere objects of evil, abstract forces of darkness. The insight that 'the constitution of the world occurs behind the backs of the individuals, yet it is their work' (Marcuse, 1988, p. 151) is turned against itself: nationalists agree that the world makes itself manifest behind the backs of what they consider as the one-national community. Yet, they deny that it is their work. Instead, it is a world of evil global forces conspiring to undermine relations of national harmony. The evil force is personified in the category 'Jew'. Capitalism becomes Jewish capitalism and globalisation a Jewish conspiracy. In the struggle between 'good' and 'evil' reconciliation appears neither possible nor desirable. Evil needs to be eradicated in order for the 'good' to be set free. The paradox of this claim seems clear, or so it seems. The attack on 'reason' rests on the employment of reason's other self: instrumental rationality, confirming, rather than denying, the circumstance that Nazism was less an aberration in the forward march of instrumental reason than the transformation of the forward march itself into delusion. The attack on reason set 'loose all irrational powers—a movement that ends with the total fictionalisation of the mind' (ibid., p. 23). Auschwitz, then, confirms the 'stubbornness' of the principle of 'abstraction' not only through extermination for extermination's sake but also, and because of it, through 'abstractification'. The biologisation of the abstract as 'Jew' denied not only humanity, as the 'Jew' stands expelled from the biologised community of the concrete. The abstract is also made abstract: all that can be used is used like teeth, hair, skin; labour-power; and, finally, the abstract is made abstract and thus invisible itself through gas. The invisible hand of the market, identified as the abstract-biological power of the 'Jew', is transformed into smoked-filled air, into the invisible itself.

Nazism's Anti-capitalist Capitalism

National Socialism projected itself as an anti-capitalist movement. This projection should not be dismissed out of hand. As the late left-wing terrorist Ulrike Meinhoff put it 'finance capital and the banks, the hard core of the system of imperialism and capitalism, had turned the hatred of men against money and exploitation, and against the Jews...Anti-Semitism is really a hatred of capitalism' (quoted in Rose, 1990, p. 304).[4] Yet, National Socialism also embraced industrial capital and new technology. Indeed, according to Aly and Heym (1988), the preparation of the Final Solution in occupied Poland was based less on anti-Semitism as an ideology, but, in fact, followed the instrumental reasoning of Neo-Malthusian resource management. Their argument is that, for the Nazis, the economic viability of occupied Poland depended on the reduction of the population per capita in order to secure that capital exported to Poland could be applied efficiently.

What is the relationship between Nazism's anti-capitalist ideological projection and the rational calculation of economic resources that proposes mass murder as a 'solution' to capitalist profitability? Nazi anti-Semitism is different from the anti-Semitism of the old Christian world. This does not mean that it did not exploit Christian anti-Semitism. Christian anti-Semitism constructed the 'Jew' as an abstract social power: The 'Jew' stands accused as the assassin of Jesus and is thus persecuted as the son of a murderer. In modern anti-Semitism, the Jew was chosen because of the 'religious horror the latter has always inspired' (Sartre, 1976, p. 68). In the Christian world, the 'Jew' was also a social-economic construct by virtue of being forced to fill the vital economic function of trafficking in money. Thus, the economic curse that this social role entailed, reinforced the religious curse.

Modern anti-Semitism uses and exploits these historical constructions and transforms them: The Jew stands accused and is persecuted for following unproductive activities. His image is that of an intellectual and banker. 'Bankers and intellectuals, money and mind, the exponents of circulation, form the impossible ideal of those who have been maimed by domination, an image used by domination to perpetuate itself' (Horkheimer and Adorno, 1989, p. 172). The biologically defined possession of land and tradition is counterposed to the possession of universal, abstract phenomena. The terms *'abstract, rationalist, intellectual*...take a pejorative sense; it could not be otherwise, since the anti-Semite lays claim to a concrete and irrational possession of the values of the nation' (Sartre, 1976, p. 109). The abstract values themselves are biologised, the abstract is identified as 'Jew'. Both, thus, the 'concrete' and the 'abstract' are biologised: one through the possession of land (the concrete as rooted in nature, blood and tradition) and the other through the possession of 'poison' (the abstract as the rootless power of intelligence and money). The myth of national unity is counterposed to the myth of the Jew. Jewry is seen to stand behind the urban world of crime, prostitution, and vulgar, materialist culture. Tradition is counterposed to reasoning, intelligence, and self-reflection; and the nationalist conception of community, economy and labour is counterposed to the abstract forces of international finance and communism (Postone, 1986). The *Volksgenossen* are thus equal in blindness. 'Anti-Semitic behaviour is generated in situations where blinded men robbed of their subjectivity are set loose as subjects' (Horkheimer and Adorno, 1989, p. 171). They were set loose as subjects of instrumental reason and are thus robbed of their subjectivity as social individuals to whom reason has and reveals meaning and significance. While reason subsists in and through the critique of social relations, the V*olksgenosse* has only faith in the efficiently unleashed terror of instrumental rationality. The collection of gold teeth from those murdered, the collection of hair from those to be killed, and the overseeing of the slave-labour of those allowed to walk on their knees for no more than another day, only requires effective organisation.

Nationalism articulates a senseless, barbaric rejection of capitalism that makes anti-capitalism useful for capitalism. 'The rulers are only safe as long as the people they rule turn their longed-for goals into hated forms of evil' (ibid., p. 199). The Jews seem ready made for the projection of horror. 'No matter what the Jews as such may be like, their image, as that of the defeated people, has the features to which totalitarian domination must be completely hostile: happiness without power, wages without work, a home without frontiers, religion without myth. These characteristics are hated by the rulers because the ruled secretly long to possess them' (ibid.). Anti-Semitism invited the ruled to stabilise domination by urging them to de-humanise, maim and kill, suppressing the very possibility and idea of happiness through their participation in the rationally organised slaughter, robbing the projected—capitalist—Others of all possession, including their life. Fascism, then, 'is also totalitarian in that it seeks to make the rebellion of suppressed nature against domination directly useful to domination. This machinery needs the Jews' (ibid., p.185). This insight poses the issue of Nazism's anti-capitalist capitalism, that is, its espousal of capitalist enterprise and its tirades against 'Jewish capitalism'. The fetish critique of capitalism as 'Jewish capitalism' argues that capitalism is in fact nothing more than an unproductive money-making system. The nation is deemed productive and capitalism is projected on to the image of the rootless 'money Jew'. This critique of global capital is based on a dualist conception between, on the one hand, social relations as relations between creative, industrious individuals and, on the other, their subordination to relations between things, to money.[5]

Marx's critique of fetishism supplied an uncompromising critique of this dualist conception by making clear that the two, use value and exchange value, industrial capital and money capital, do not exist independent from each other but are in fact each other's mode of existence. The critique of capital has to be a critique of economic categories, and that is, a critique of the fetishism of the commodity form which entails the exploitation of labour and the form of money as its presupposition. Without such a critique, it is all too easy to succumb to the objective delusion that the commodity form presents. On the one hand, there is the separation of reality into concrete matter and abstract destructive force, leading to the fetish-like endorsement of the concrete, of creative enterprise and of industry supplying material products that satisfy wants. On the other hand, there is the abstract sphere occupied by money and finance, specifically speculation and global finance capital. The celebration of the concrete goes hand-in-hand with the rejection of the mobility, universality and intangibility of finance capital that is charged with knowing neither national identity nor national 'responsibility'. The Vampire-like figure of capital sucking labour in the quest for surplus value, portrayed by Marx in *Capital*, is thus displaced: the Vampire becomes money. Industrial enterprise, rather than being conceived in terms of an enterprise of exploitation, is projected as the 'national laboratory' of concrete, creative labour. It is projected as a national community where national labour is employed in the much praised one-national boat. The viability of this labour is seen to be threatened by money. Money is conceived as the root of all evil and the cause of all perversion. Enterprise and industry are fetishised as concrete community, as concrete nature. National industrial endeavour is thus portrayed as a 'victim' of the evil forces of abstract values, of money. In sum, modern anti-Semitism is the barbaric ideology of what Marx (1966, p. 438) described in his analysis of the role of credit as the 'abolition of the capitalist mode of production within the capitalist mode of production itself'. National Socialism focuses the resolution of this negative abolition on the national state as the 'harmonies' last refuge' (Marx, 1973, p. 886) that restores in the face of global economic turmoil, the alleged 'national interest' in the exploitation of labour through terror.

For the anti-Semites, the world appears to be divided between finance capital and concrete nature. The concrete is conceived as immediate, direct, matter for use, and rooted in industry and productive activity. Money, on the other hand, is not only conceived as the root of all evil, it is also judged as rootless and of existing not only independently from industrial capital but, also, over and against the industrial endeavour of the nation: all enterprise is seen to be perverted in the name of money's continued destructive quest for self-expansion. In this way, money and financial capital are identified with capitalism while industry is perceived as constituting the concrete and creative enterprise of a national community. Between capitalism as monetary accumulation and national community as industrial enterprise, it is money which calls the shots. In this view, industry and enterprise are 'made' capitalist by money: money penetrates all expressions of industry and thus perverts and disintegrates community in the name of finance capital's abstract values. This destructive force puts claim on and so perverts: the individual as entrepreneur; the creative in terms of a paternalist direction of use-value production; the rooted in terms of *Volk*; the community in terms of a natural community. Instead of community's natural order of hierarchy and position, money's allegedly artificial and rootless force is judged to make the world go round by uprooting the natural order of the *Volksgenossen*. In this way, then, it is possible for the *Volksgenossen* not only to embrace capitalism but, also, to declare that the exploitation of labour creates freedom: *Arbeit macht frei*. 'They declared that work was not degrading, so as to control the others more rationally. They claimed to be creative workers, but in reality they were still the grasping overlords of former times' (Horkheimer and Adorno, 1989, p. 173). By separating what fundamentally belongs together, that is 'industrial' exploitation and money, the differentiation between money on the one hand, and industry and enterprise, on the other, amounts to a fetish critique of capital that attacks the projected personifications of capital rather than the capitalist relations of exploitation themselves.

With the biologisation of creative activity, the unfettered operation of the exploitation of labour in the name mythologised concrete values is rendered attainable by the elimination of the cajoling and perverting forces of the abstract—the 'money Jew'. In this way, the ideology of blood and soil, on the one hand, and machinery and unfettered industrial expansion, on the other, are projected as images of a healthy nation that stands ready to purge itself from the perceived perversion of industry by the abstract, universal, rootless, mobile, intangible, international 'vampire' of 'Jewish capitalism'. The celebration of the *Volksgenosse* as the personification of the concrete, of blood, soil, tradition and industry, allows the killing of Jews without fear. Yet, it manifests 'the stubbornness of the life to which one has to conform, and to resign oneself' (ibid., p. 171): the idle occupation of killing is efficiently discharged.

Everything is thus changed into pure nature. The abstract was not only personalised and biologised, it was also 'abstractified'. Auschwitz was a factory 'to destroy the personification of the abstract. Its organisation was that of a fiendish industrial process, the aim of which was to "liberate" the concrete from the abstract. The first step was to dehumanise, that is, to strip away the "mask" of humanity, of qualitative specificity, and reveal the Jews for what "they really are"—shadows, ciphers, numbered abstraction'. Then followed the process to 'eradicate that abstractness, to transform it into smoke, trying in the process to wrest away the last remnants of the concrete material "use-values": clothes, gold, hair, soap' (Postone, 1986, pp. 313-14).

Conclusion

Adam Smith was certain that capitalism creates the wealth of nations and noted that 'the proprietor of stock is properly a citizen of the world, and is not necessarily attached to any particular country. He would be apt to abandon the country in which he was exposed to a vexatious inquisition, in order to be assessed to a burdensome tax, and would remove his stock to some other country where he could either carry on his business, or enjoy his fortune more at his ease' (1981, pp. 848-49). Ricardo concurred, adding that 'if a capital is not allowed to get the greatest net revenue that the use of machinery will afford here, it will be carried abroad' leading to 'serious discouragement to the demand for labour' (Ricardo, 1995, p. 39). According to Hegel, the accumulation of wealth renders those who depend on the sale of their labour power for their social reproduction, insecure in deteriorating conditions. He concluded that despite the accumulation of wealth, bourgeois society will find it most difficult to keep the dependent masses pacified, and he saw the form of the state as the means of reconciling the social antagonism, containing the dependent masses. Ricardo formulated the necessity of capitalist social relations to produce 'redundant population'. Marx developed this insight and showed that the idea of 'equal rights' in principle is a bourgeois right (cf. Marx, 1968). Against the bourgeois form of formal equality, he argued that communism rests on the equality of individual human needs. Adorno and Horkheimer argued that anti-Semitism is a fetishistic, barbaric critique of capitalism that makes the hatred of capitalism functional for capitalism. Luxemburg argued that the fight against barbarism is a fight for socialism.

The history of capitalism shows that the so-called golden age of the capitalism of the 1950s was an exception, if indeed it was golden at all. It did not come about as a result of either cosmopolitan reason or commitments to redistributive justice. As Gambino (1996) has shown, Fascism and Nazism were not in their origins the losing versions of Fordism, but were forced to become such thanks to the class struggles of the 1930s in the United States.[6] This struggle is the practical question of our time.

What is the contemporary meaning of this question? 'The renunciation of internationalism in the name of resurgent nationalism' is the biggest danger (Clarke, 2001, p. 91). 'Anti-globalisation' gives in to reactionary forces if its critique of globalisation is a critique for the national state. The history of protectionism, national self-sufficiency and 'national money' has always been a world market history (Bonefeld, 2000)—there are however disturbing exceptions like, for example, Albania during the Cold War and North Korea. The critique of globalisation in favour of 'national socialism' merely offers, whether intentionally or not, the horrors of the past to the present as a solution.

The idea of saving capitalism through institutional reform from its own self-destructive dynamic has to be exposed to reveal its meaning and that is, that money must manage and organise the exploitation of labour. What is the opposite term to the unfettered global accumulation of capital? Is the opposing term the national state that, with transformed regulative powers, forces capital to guarantee the common national good? The ethical appeal of the demand for regulative transformation resides in its critical comparison between the less than perfect reality of capitalist relations and the pleasant norms of equality and justice. Such critical comparison fails to see that the pleasant norms are adequate to their content, the bad reality of a capitalist mode of production. The much desired benevolent regulation of capital presupposes inhuman conditions and these find a political expression in the form of the state which Marx summarised as: 'the concentration of bourgeois society'. Discontent with—neoliberal—politicians amounts to, paraphrasing Marx, a critique of charactermasks, deflecting from the social constitution of their existence and because of this, it affirms the state as if it were an 'independent being which possesses its own *intellectual, ethical and libertarian bases*' (Marx, 1968, p. 28). It thus amounts to a mere rebellion for a virtuous state—a state, that is, which secures the 'communal interests' of bourgeois society, that is, capitalist accumulation.

Last, the critique of globalisation fails if it is merely a critique of speculative capital and that is, a critique for productive accumulation. It was the crisis of productive accumulation that sustained the divorce of monetary accumulation from productive accumulation (Bonefeld and Holloway, 1996). Globalisation is not responsible for the ever more precarious conditions of work, poverty, and debt, and the ever more destructive force of speculation. Rather, and as Daniel Cohen (1997, p. 15) has argued, it is the restructuring of work that makes globalisation possible and gives globalisation a bad name. This then means that 'anti-globalisation' has to be a critique of the capitalistically constituted relations of production. The critique of, for example, the WTO is not enough. Trade, whether deemed fair or unfair, presupposes capitalist relations of exploitation. Further, without the critique of exploitation, the critique of speculation leads with necessity to xenophobia and anti-Semitic denunciations of money. It conceals the relations of exploitation and is complicit, whether intentionally or not, in the critique of finance as parasitic. Racism and Nazi anti-Semitism shows what that means.

The rejection of the bourgeois relations of abstract equality in favour of nationalist conceptions of equality is reactionary. This is the law of abstract equality: 'The power which each individual exercises over the activity of others or over social wealth exists in him as the owner of *exchange value*, of *money*. The individual carries his social power, as well as his bond with society, in his pocket' (Marx, 1973, pp. 156-57). And the law of the national equality of a people? It is racist. The critique of abstract equality has to be an anti-national critique and that is, a critique of capital and its state—the political master of the national homogenisation of human relations as mere personifications of relations between things.

The theoretical and practical orientation on the utopia of the society of the free and equal is the only realistic departure from the inhumanity that the world market society of capital posits (cf. Agnoli, 2000). In short, those who seriously want freedom and equality as social individuals but do not wish to destabilise capitalism and instead wish to regulate 'abstractions', be it capital or the market, contradict themselves. The attempt to regulate abstractions affirms their constituted existence and thus renders them effective. The struggle for socialism is a struggle against abstractions—and 'abstractifications'—and that is, a struggle for the equality of individual human needs. Paraphrasing Marx (1959, p. 93), 'it is precisely necessary to avoid ever again to counterpose "society" as an abstraction, to the individual'.

Anti-capitalism has, thus, to mean anti-capitalism. It has to mean the complete democratisation of all social forces, making them accountable to individual human needs in and through the democratic organisation of socially necessary labour by the freely associated producers themselves, where the free development of each is the condition for the free development of all. 'Every emancipation is a restoration of the human world and of human relationships to *Man* [*Menschen*] *himself*' (Marx, 1964, p. 370).

The democratic organisation of economic relations of

necessity and the reduction of labour time belong together as each other's presupposition. How much labour time was needed in 2002 to produce the same amount of commodities that was produced in 1992? Twenty per cent? Forty per cent or fifty per cent? Whatever the percentage might be, what is certain is that labour time has not decreased. It has increased. What is certain too is that the distribution of wealth is as unequal as never before. And how does bourgeois society cope with the expansion of 'redundant populations', on the one hand, and, on the other, the overaccumulation of abstract wealth, of capital? The contradiction between the forces and relations of production does seek resolution: destruction of productive forces, scrapping of labour through war and generalised poverty and misery, the racist demand for national equality, and all this against the background of an unprecedented accumulation of wealth and the ever more destructive attempts to valorise atoms of time through greater labour flexibility.

Anti-capitalist indifference to the revolutionary project of human emancipation is a contradiction in terms. Such contradictions seek resolution and the grotesque and bloody grimace of the last century shows what that might mean. The 20th century has been a lousy century. It was filled with dogmas that one after another have cost us time and suffering. It would, however, be wrong to see it in this one-sided way. It was also a century of hope in the alternative entelechy of solidarity and human emancipation—from Mexico (1914) to Petrograd (1917) and Kronstadt (1921), from Berlin (1918), Budapest (1919) and Barcelona (1936) to Budapest (1956), from Paris (1968), Chiapas (1994) to the Argentinean *piqueteros* (2001).[7] These, and many more, have been the intense moments of human emancipation, constituting points of departure towards the society of the free and equal.

In conclusion, anti-capitalism has to demand the democratic organisation of socially necessary labour time by the associated producers themselves. This, then, is the splendid category of full employment in and through the emancipation of labour that Marx conceived as the democratic organisation of necessity through the realm of freedom: human self-determination, human sovereignty, and thus human dignity. Anti-capitalist indifference to the project of human emancipation does not pose an alternative to capitalism. It succumbs to abstractions, deprives itself of the weapon of reason, and leaves the door open to socialism's alternative, that is, barbarism. Anti-capitalism has to mean the organised negation of capital and its state, that is, it has to espouse the categorical imperative of human emancipation.

NOTES

1. On this the exchange between de Angelis, Bonefeld and Zarembka in *The Commoner* (www.commoner.org.uk).
2. Quoted in 'Malaysia Acts on Market Fall', *Financial Times*, September 4, 1997.
3. For a recent diatribe, see Buchanan's (2002) Aryan dream of a white fortress America that he sees to be in crisis because of the nefarious effects of 'critical theory' for which holds 'those trouble making Communist Jews' responsible.
4. Rose's book offers a conventional conservative critique of revolutionary thought. For a thorough critique of left-wing anti-Semitism, see IFS (2000).
5. This part draws on Postone (1986).
6. As Gambino put it, 'the assembly line is, together with totalitarian state systems and racist nationalism, one of the originating structures which broadly explain the concentration-camp crimes perpetrated on an industrial scale'. The history of so-called Fordism is often seen as a phase where capitalism took on reforming itself in a social-democratic manner. However, as Gambino emphasises, 'Fascism and Nazism were not in their origins the losing versions of Fordism, but were forced to become such thanks to the social and working-class struggles of the 1930s in the United States' (p. 48).
7. For a conceptualisation of the means and ends of human emancipation, see the collection of essays published in Bonefeld and Tischler (2002).

REFERENCES

Adorno, T. (1951), *Minima Moralia*. Frankfurt: Surhkamp.

Adorno, T. (1969), 'Erziehung nach Auschwitz', in ibid., *Stichworte. Kritische Modelle* 2. Frankfurt: Suhrkamp.

Adorno, T. (1990), *Negative Dialectics*. London: Routledge.

Agnoli, J. (1997), *Faschismus ohne Revision*. Freiburg: Ça ira.

Agnoli, J. (2000), 'The Market, the State and the End of History', in Bonefeld, W. and K. Psychopedis (eds.).

Agnoli, J. (2002), 'Emancipation: Paths and Goals', in Bonefeld, W. and S. Tischler (eds.).

Aly, G. and S. Heym (1988), 'The Economics of the Final Solution', *Simon Wiesenthal Centre Annual, no. 5.*

Bonefeld, W. (2000), 'The Spectre of Globalisation', in Bonefeld, W. and K. Psychopedis (eds.).

Bonefeld, W. and J. Holloway (eds.) (1996), *Global Capital, National State and the Politics of Money*. London: Macmillan.

Bonefeld, W. and K. Psychopedis (eds.) (2000), *The Politics of Change*. London: Palgrave.

Bonefeld, W. and S. Tischler (eds.) (2002), *What is to be Done?* Aldershot: Ashgate.

Buchanan, P. (2002), *The Death of the West*. New York: Dunne.

Callinicos, A. (2003), 'The Anti-Globalisation Movement after Genoa and New York', in Aronowitz, S. and H. Gautney (eds.) *Implicating Empire*. New York: Basic Books.

Clarke, S. (1992), 'The Global Accumulation of Capital and the Periodisation of the Capitalist State Form', in Bonefeld, W. et al (eds.) *Open Marxism*. Vol. I, London: Pluto.

Clarke, S. (2001), 'Class Struggle and the Global Overaccumulation of Capital', in Albritton, R. et al (eds.), *Phases of Capitalist Development*. London: Palgrave.

Cohen, D. (1997), *Fehldiagnose Globalisierung*. Frankfurt: Campus.

Gambino, F. (1996), 'A Critique of the Fordism of the Regulation School', *Common Sense*, No. 19.

Horkheimer, M. (1988), 'Die Juden in Europa', in *Schriften 1936-1941*, Vol. 4, Frankfurt: Fischer.

Horkheimer, M. and T. Adorno (1989), *Dialectic of Enlightenment*. London: Verso.

IFS (2000), Initiative Sozialistisches Forum, *Furchbare Anti-Semiten, ehrbare Antizionisten*. Freiburg: Ça ira.

Lyotard, J.F. (1993), *Political Writings*. London: University College London Press.

Marable, M. (1991), *Race Reform and Rebellion*. 2nd ed., Jackson: University Press of Mississippi.

Marcuse, H. (1988), *Negations*. London: Free Association Press.

Marx, K. (1959), *Economic and Philosophical Manuscripts of 1844*. London: Lawrence & Wishart.

Marx, K. (1962), *Das Kapital*. Vol. I, Berlin: Dietz.

Marx, K. (1964), *Zur Judenfrage*. MEW 1, Berlin: Dietz.

Marx, K. (1968), *Kritik des Gothaer Programms*. MEW 19, Berlin: Dietz.

Marx, K. (1966), *Capital*. Vol. III, London: Lawrence & Wishart.

Marx, K. (1973), *Grundrisse*. London: Penguin.

Marx, K. (1975), 'Contribution to the Critique of Hegel's Philosophy of Law. Introduction', *Collected Works*. Vol. 3, London: Lawrence & Wishart.

Marx, K. and F. Engels (1996), *The Communist Manifesto*. London: Pluto.

Negt, O. (2001), *Arbeit und menschliche Würde*. Göttingen: Steidl.

Postone, M. (1986), 'Anti-Semitism and National Socialism', in Rabinbach, A. and J. Zipes (eds.) (1986), *Germans and Jews Since the Holocaust*. New York: Holmes & Meier.

Reichelt, H. (2002), 'Die Marxsche Kritik "konomisher Kategorien', in Fetscher, I. and A. Schmidt (eds.) *Emanzipation als Versoehnung*. Frankfurt: Verlag Neue Kritik.

Ricardo, D. (1995), *On the Principles of Political Economy and Taxation*. Cambridge: Cambridge University Press.

Rose, P.L. (1990), *German Question/Jewish Question*. Princeton: Princeton University Press.

Sartre, J-P. (1976), *Anti-Semite and Jew*. New York: Schocken.

Sohn-Rhethel, A. (1970), *Geistige und koerperliche Arbeit*. Frankfurt: Suhrkamp.

Smith, A. (1981), *The Wealth of Nations*. Vol. II, Indianapolis: Liberty Fund.

2

History and Human Emancipation: Struggle, Uncertainty, and Openness

'All emancipation is the restoration of the human world and of human relationships to Man himself' (Marx).

'Class' is not an affirmative category but a critical concept. The critique of class society finds the positive only in the classless society, in communism. Communism means 'communis'—the commune or association of the direct producers, where each contributes according to her abilities, and where each receives according to her needs. This, then, is the society of the free and equal—a commune of communist individuals who exercise their own social power directly.[1] Instead of counter-posing 'society' as an abstraction to the individual, the communist individuals recognise and organise 'society' as their own social product.

Class analysis is therefore not a flag-waving exercise on behalf of the working class. Indeed, 'to be a productive labourer is...not a piece of luck, but a misfortune.'[2] Affirmative conceptions of class, however well-meaning and benevolent in their intensions, presuppose the working class as a productive force that deserves a better, a new deal. What is a fair wage? Marx made the point that '"price of labour" is just as irrational as a yellow logarithm'.[3] The demand for fair wages and fair labour conditions abstracts from the very conditions of 'fairness' in capitalism. Marx's insight according to which 'a great deal of capital, which appears today in the United States without any certificate of birth, was yesterday, in England, the capitalised blood of children', remains a powerful judgement on contemporary conditions of capitalistically constituted fair and equal exchange relations.[4]

Theory on behalf of the working class leads to the acceptance of programmes and tickets whose common basis is the everyday religion of bourgeois society: commodity fetishism. Chapter 48 of Volume Three of *Capital* provides Marx's critique of the theory of class proposed by classical political economy (and shared by modern social science), according to which class interests are determined by the revenue sources (or, in Weberian terms, market situation) of social groups, rather than being founded in the social relations of production as Marx argues.[5] Political Economy is indeed a scholarly dispute how the booty pumped out of the labourer may be divided[6] —and clearly, the more the labourer gets, the better. After all, it is her social labour that produces the 'wealth of nations'. Even on the assumption that when hiring labour, equivalent is exchanged for equivalent, 'the transaction is all that only the old dodge of every conqueror who buys commodities from the conquered with the money he has robbed them of'.[7] The critique of political economy is not satisfied with perpetuating the labourer. Its reasoning is subversive of all relations of human indignity. Subversion is not the business of alternative elites that seek revolution as a mere conformist rebellion—a revolution for the perpetuation of wage slavery. Their business is to lead labour, not its self-emancipation. Subversion aims at general human emancipation.

History does not make history

The second and third Internationals subscribed to naturalised conceptions of society and history. Their equally 'naturalised Marxism' argued that capitalist economic categories have a trans-historical validity, that distinct modes of production are distinguished by the way in which these categories manifest themselves in historically concrete societies, and that history contained a objective developmental logic, which in critical expansion of Smith's stages theory of history, moves relentlessly through the ages until transition to socialism becomes an 'objective possibility'. The revisionists did so to argue that revolution was unnecessary, and the orthodoxy that revolution was a product of natural necessity.[8] I am not at all certain that history contains this teleology and note that erstwhile proponents of this view, see for example Wolfgang-Fritz Haug, now think so too, declaring that such belief in the objective necessity of state socialist transformation has revealed itself as a 'child's dream'.[9] If, however, history is not the consequence of either divine revelation or abstract historical laws, what is it?

History does not make history. That is to say, '[h]istory does nothing, does not "possess vast wealth", does not "fight battles"! It is Man, rather, the real, living Man who does all that, who does possess and fight, it is not "history" that uses Man [*Mensch*] as a means to pursue its ends, as if it were a person apart. History is nothing but the activity of Man pursuing its ends'.[10] Historical materialism is not the dogma indicated by clever opponents and unthinking proponents alike, but a critique of things understood as dogmatic. That is to say, the 'human anatomy contains a key to the anatomy of the ape', but not conversely, the anatomy of the ape does not explain the anatomy of Man.[11] If the anatomy of the ape would really explain the anatomy of Man than the ape would already possess Man as the innate necessity of its evolution—a natural teleology or an already written future. The future, however, has not already been written. Nor will it be the result of some abstractly supposed objective logic of historical development. History does not unfold, as if it were a person apart. History has to be made, and will be made, by Man pursuing her ends. The future that will come will not result from some objective laws of historical development but will result from the struggles of today. The orthodox argument about the objective laws of historical development does not reveal abstract historical laws. It reveals accommodation to 'objective conditions', and derives socialism from capitalism, not as an alternative but as its supposedly more effective competitor.

There is no universal historical law that leads human kind from some imagined historical beginning via capitalism to socialism. Neither is history on the side of the working class. History takes no sides: it can as easily be the history of barbarism as of socialism—yet, against the background of three decades of sustained attack on the working class, and in the face of terror, war, global financial meltdown and—the threat of—global depression, barbarism seems the more likely alternative, and it seems more likely today than only yesterday. Yet, the fact that monetary accumulation (M...M') is dissociated from productive accumulation (M...P...M') is testimony to the radicality of the challenge to capitalist power, and of the fear that follows from it that every upturn in the economy would reactivate conflict.[12] Over the last 25 years, capitalism created its own virtual reality, accumulating fictitious wealth, mortgaging the future exploitation of labour. This mortgage has now broken down. The pace of crisis-ridden change in the world has accelerated to such a degree that a considered judgement on the future is quite impossible. Nevertheless, and especially in the misery of our time, it is worth recalling Marx's insight that 'all social life is essentially practical'. Just imagine, I say that contemporary conditions make revolution impossible, and then it breaks out, say, in Paderborn or Mainz of all places!

Objective Condition—what is that?

Man has to eat. This is a natural necessity, from which derives neither capitalism nor socialism. To say that capitalist economic categories are categories of natural necessity, entails not only the naturalisation of essentially social categories and therewith also the ontologisation of capitalist economic categories as self-active things, that, posited by nature, appear to develop according to their own innate logic, as developed nature. Such naturalisation of social categories also entails the derivation of class struggle from assumed structural properties. This, then, is the argument that objective laws of development structure the behaviour and actions of social classes and set the general framework within which class struggle unfolds. Joachim Hirsch has formulated this point succinctly when he argued that '*within the framework* of its general laws, capitalist development is determined ... by the actions of the acting subjects and classes, the resulting concrete conditions of crisis and their political consequences'.[13] That is to say, the laws of social existence impose themselves 'objectively' on the backs of the protagonists.[14] It is true that in capitalism, the constitution of the world occurs behind the backs of the individuals, yet—critically—it is their work. This approach, then, represses the whole issue of social-historical constitution. Instead, it elevates the 'laws' of second nature, the existence of which depended on the continued existence of specific social relations, into general historical laws.[15]

Louis Althusser, who needs to be credited with transforming Soviet Marxism into an academically viable branch of Western Marxism, could therefore argue that the critique of political economy is not a critique of capitalism but that it rather 'develops the conceptual system' of scientific Marxism.[16] According to Althusser and his school, it shows the capitalist anatomy of trans-historical laws of economic necessity but does not analyse capitalism as a living process. Deciphering the natural basis of the capitalist mode of production requires therefore microscopic attention, abstracting the enduring structures of economic necessity from their over-determined mode of historical appearance, of their capitalist substantiation. Struggle for socialism would thus require not only a revolutionary vanguard in the form of the party, but also a scientific vanguard that, independent from tactical and strategic struggles, provides socialism with scientific insight into economic nature, including the technical knowledge that the regulation of a socialist economy of labour requires. The orthodox endeavour to trace capitalist social categories to their trans-historical natural basis says more than it cares to admit. On closer inspection its endeavour seems in every respect tied to capitalist realities, including its conception of progress. By naturalising capitalist categories, it elevates them into laws of history in general. It thus represents history as a history of capitalism's becoming, and conceives of socialism as a derivative of capitalism.[17] That is to say, and drawing on Marx's critique of the 'economists'' naturalisation of economic categories, it presents the capitalist mode of production as 'encased in eternal natural laws independent of history'. It is this presentation that allows them, the economists and scientific socialists, to smuggle capitalist relations in as the 'inviolable natural laws on which society and history in the abstract are founded'.[18] There is no such thing as abstract history. History does not make history.

In distinction to the second and third Internationals and its benevolent academicians and resourceful technocrats, capitalist economic categories do not have a trans-historical validity. They belong to the society from which they spring. Capitalist laws of social reproduction are finite, transient products of the finite and transient reality of capitalism. Whether the struggle for human emancipation goes beyond these categories is a matter of communist social practice. Nature, or the so-called objective laws of historical development, has nothing to do with it. That is to say, the future has not already been written, social structures are valid only for and within human social relations, capitalist economic categories manifest the laws of necessity in capitalistically constituted forms of social relations, which 'Men have entered into' historically,[19] and history does not impose itself objectively on the acting subjects, as if it were a person apart. History does not happen by itself. Whatever history there will be, it will have been made by the acting subjects themselves. The future is made in the present, it is as much a present-future as a future-present.

In capitalism, every progress turns into a calamity

The working class struggles not because of Marx's critique of political economy, but because it is an exploited and dominated class. It struggled against capitalism before Marx put pen to paper, and struggles against capitalism until this day not because but despite Marx. One could argue, as indeed Johannes Agnoli has, that it is 'Man, who, as a single individual, as a group, or as a mass, understands himself as subject and who defends himself against a merely objective existence—in politics, in religion, in philosophy. One can say that subversion is a truly human phenomenon. Man objects to be a mere football of the almighty. Here he is a mere object. Similarly, as a servant of the master he is a mere object, regardless of whether we conceive this in social or religious terms. Man is never at the centre of politics (as the political parties say), but he is a means of politics...And an object he remains most of all when he is kept in a state of ignorance...Subversion operates against systems of thought, against political and economic systems, that threaten nature and therewith always also Man'.[20] Subversion is able to negate the established order because it is 'man' made.

Marx's relevance to contemporary class struggle is simply this: his critique of political economy reveals the genesis of existing social relations in human practice—this at least is its critical intention—, and his argument shows that existing relations of misery develop by force of their negation: in order to posit surplus labour capital has to posit necessary labour. The '*relation between necessary labour and surplus labour*...is... the relation between the constitutive parts of the working day and the class relation which constitutes it'.[21] Capital depends on the imposition of necessary labour, the constituent side of surplus labour, upon the world's working classes. It has to posit necessary labour at the same time as which it has to reduce necessary labour to the utmost in order to increase surplus value. This reduction develops labour's productive power. That is, less social labour time is needed to produce an equivalent amount of use-values. Increased labour productivity tends thus to increase material wealth. The circumstance that less and less socially necessary labour time is required to produce, for want of a better expression, the necessities of life, limits the realm of necessity and so allows the blossoming of what Marx characterised as the realm of freedom.[22] Yet, given the capitalist form of wealth, this increase in 'material wealth may correspond to a simultaneous fall in the magnitude of its value'.[23] Accumulation for the sake of accumulation thus tends to push the capitalist mode of production beyond the limits of its social form. Containing it within its form requires force (*Gewalt*), including not only the destruction of productive capacities, unemployment, but also the destruction of human life through war and ecological disaster. Every social progress turns into a calamity. In capitalism, every increase in labour productivity shortens the hours of labour but in its capitalist form, it lengthens them. The introduction of sophisticated machinery lightens labour but in its capitalist form, it heightens the intensity of labour. Every increase in the productivity of labour increases the material wealth of the producers but in its capitalist form makes them paupers. Most importantly of all, greater labour productivity sets labour free, makes labour redundant. But rather then shortening the hours of work and thus absorbing all labour into production on the basis of a shorter working day, freeing life-time from the 'realm of necessity', those in employment are exploited more intensively, while those made redundant find themselves on the scrap heap of a mode of production that sacrifices '"human machines" on the pyramids of accumulation'[24] .

There is only one human measure that cannot be modified. It can only be lost (Max Frisch)

The class struggle over the capitalist attempt at reducing the workers' life-time (*Lebenszeit*) to work-time, takes place in the hidden abode of production, behind the factory gate on which is written 'no entry except on business'. Is this a struggle between mere agents or bearers (*Träger*) of objective economic laws and structures? Unsurprisingly, the bourgeoisie endorses this notion of the working class, and demands that it behaves well as a bearer of economic resourcefulness, that is, as a compliant, effective, efficient and resourceful factor of production. It also tells the working class to tie its interests to the expanded accumulation of capital so that it obtains its just reward by means of the so-called trickle down effect. However, for itself, the bourgeoisie rejects such notions. Instead it demands respect and celebration of its purposefulness and overall humanity. The saying that Man is by nature lazy tells us nothing about human nature. However, it tells us a lot about bourgeois society. There is no doubting the fact that quite a few of those who have never worked have historically been wined and dined rather well. The supposition that the working class lacks humanity because in reality it is just a productive agent reveals therefore a certain class standpoint.[25]

The orthodox tradition of Western Marxism belittles the idea that society has to do with Menschen in their social relations of production. Louis Althusser argued that one can recognise Man only on the condition that the philosophical myth of Man is reduced to ash. Nicos Poulantzas radicalised this view when he argued that Marx's theory amounts to a radical break from the 'historical problematic of the subject'.[26] Althusser was however right to argue that Man does not exist. In the topsy turvey world of capital, Man exists indeed as a personification of economic categories. However, does it therefore follow that the critique of political economy is really no more than a secularised mythology of the 'logic of things'? Does it really make sense to say that workers personify variable capital? Variable does not go on strike. Workers do. Wherever capital goes, capitalist class conflict occurs, and wherever class conflict occurs, capital seeks flight, though not always successfully.[27]

The emancipation of the working class can only be achieved by the working class itself. But how? The simple idea of human emancipation is difficult to conceive in practice. According to Georg Lukács the worker can resist reification because, as long as he rebels against it consciously, 'his humanity and his soul are not changed into commodities' (Lukács, 1970, p. 172). Lukács derives the revolutionary subject, he calls it the totality of the proletarian subject represented by the party, from the humanity and soul of the worker—the party is the soul and presents the humanity of the otherwise reified worker. Ernst Bloch (2000) talks about the 'inner transcendence of matter'; Oskar Negt and Alexander Kluge (1993) about 'materialist instinct', and Antonio Negri (and his co-author Michael Hardt) about the bio-power of the multitude.[28] These differentiations of society into system and soul/transcendent matter/materialist instinct/bio-power separate what belongs together. Indeed, whichever formulation is favoured, they all insist on a subject that is conceived in contradistinction to society—all seem to favour a subject that possesses either a theological (soul), material or biological residue that as the (invisible) essence of resistance has not been fully absorbed by capitalism.

The theologised or biologised subject is not a social subject. It is an asserted subject. It is meant to do what the antagonistic society is no longer assumed to be able to do, that is, to realise the social subject in battle against its own perverted mode of existence. Really? It is quite possible that the history as we know it has come to an end. 'Of one thing we can be certain. The ideologies of the 20th century will disappear completely. This has been a lousy century. It has been filled with dogmas, dogmas that one after another have cost us time, suffering, and much injustice'.[29] For every history that comes to an end another history comes to the fore. The 20th century was also a century of hope in the alternative entelechy of solidarity and human emancipation—from Mexico (1914) to Petrograd (1917) and Kronstadt (1921), Berlin (1918), Budapest (1919) and Barcelona (1936) to Berlin (1953) and Budapest (1956), from Paris (1968), Gdansk (1980) Chiapas (1994) to the Argentinean *piqueteros* (2001).[30] These, and many more, have been the intense moments of the struggle for human social autonomy, constituting points of departure towards the society of the free and equal.

Realism and class struggle

The difficulty of conceiving of the self-emancipation of the working class has to do with the very idea of human emancipation. In distinction to the pursuit of profit, seizure of the state, pursuit and preservation of political power, and economic value and human resource, it follows a completely different entelechy of human development. Quite reasonably, the labour movement strives for the so-called emancipation of labour and concerns itself—commendably—with the improvement of the quality of life for workers. There is however more to this concern than it appears on first sight.

There is thus need for a realistic conception of the struggle for human emancipation. Class struggle has to be rediscovered as the laboratory of communism—this movement of the working class in and against capitalism. This struggle does not follow some abstract idea. Nor does it target capitalist society from some sort of external vantage point. Class struggle is a struggle in and against capitalism. Its dynamic tends to push beyond institutionalised forms of class incorporation and regulation. Whether it does can neither be predicted nor organised from above. That is to say, class-consciousness cannot be brought to the workers from without—the communist party does not commandeer the unconscious. It is partial to the class struggle. In this, the communists 'express the actual relations springing from an existing class struggle, form a historical movement going on under our very eyes'[31] The idea that workers lack class-consciousness entails not only the notion of the Party as the vanguard bearer of that consciousness. It entails also the accusation that workers lack understanding of what is best for them, and that they therefore need to be led. This justification of the form of the party rests on the so-called objective character of conditions. According to this view, the working class is the revolutionary class because of its objective position in the production process. It is by virtue of its 'objective' position that the working class is the revolutionary class. Objective does not mean subjective. That is, objectively, the working class exists in-itself and, in order to realise its potential as a revolutionary class, it has to be transformed into a class for-itself, into a class subject. This transformation requires 'leadership'. 'In-itself' the working class can only develop economic consciousness, not political consciousness. Class in-itself thus means that its consciousness is tied to capitalist realities, and that in-itself the working class is unable to look beyond capitalism. What however is the working class 'in-itself' struggling for?

'In-itself' the working class struggles for better wages and conditions, and defends wage levels and conditions. It struggles against capital's 'were-wolf's hunger for surplus labour' and its destructive conquest for additional atoms of labour-time, and thus against its reduction to a mere time's carcass.[32] It struggles against a life constituting solely of labour-time and thus against a reduction of her human life to a mere economic resource. It struggles for respect, education, and recognition of human significance, and above all it struggles for food, shelter, clothing, warmth, love, affection, knowledge, and dignity. It struggles against the reduction of its life-time to labour-time, of its humanity to an economic resource, of its living existence to personified labour-time. Its struggle as a class 'in-itself' really is a struggle 'for-itself': for life, human distinction, life-time, and above all, satisfaction of basic human needs. It does all of this in conditions (*Zustände*) in which the increase in material wealth that it has produced, pushes beyond the limits of the capitalist form of wealth.[33] Every so-called trickle down effect that capitalist accumulation might bring forth presupposes a prior and sustained trickle up in the capitalist accumulation of wealth. And then society 'suddenly finds itself put back into a state of momentary barbarism; it appears as if famine, a universal war of devastation had cut off the supply of every means of subsistence; industry and commerce seem to be destroyed; and why? Because there is too much civilisation, too much means of subsistence; too much industry, too much commerce. The productive forces at the disposal of society no longer tend to further the development of the conditions of bourgeois property; on the contrary, they have become too powerful for these conditions, by which they are fettered, and so soon as they overcome these fetters, they bring disorder into the whole of bourgeois society, endanger the existence of bourgeois property. The conditions of bourgeois society are too narrow to comprise the wealth created by them. And how does bourgeois society get over these crises? On the one hand by enforced destruction of a mass of productive forces; on the other, by the conquest of new markets, and by the more thorough exploitation of the old ones.[34] In conclusion, 'freedom is a hollow delusion for as long as one class of humans can starve another with impunity. Equality is a hollow delusion for as long as the rich exercise the right to decide over the life and death of others'.[35] The existence of the labourer as an economic category does therefore not entail reduction of consciousness to economic consciousness. It entails the concept of economy as an experienced concept, and economic consciousness as an experienced consciousness. At the very least, economic consciousness is an unhappy consciousness.[36] It is this consciousness that demands reconciliation: freedom turns concrete in the changing forms of repression as resistance to repression.

The understanding of class struggle has thus to be brought down, away from the 'lofty' sphere of scientistic supposition of 'objective conditions' and 'objective laws of historical development', and towards 'the real life-activity' of the real individuals, their activity and the conditions under which they live.[37] What needs to be attained, then, is a conception of struggle that is in keeping with the insight that for the oppressed 'the "state of emergency" in which we live, is not the exception but the rule'.[38] Upon reaching the factory gate with its inscription 'no entry except on business', one has to enter to appreciate the daily struggle over the reduction of the worker to personified labour-time, over the appropriation of atoms of additional labour time. This also entails that instead of succumbing to the imaginary of globalisation as some sort of deterritorialised and dematerialised cyber-space, it would make sense to develop a conception of struggle that understands that the 'everyday struggle over the production and appropriation of surplus value in every individual workplace and every local community...is the basis of the class struggle on a global scale'.[39] The world's proletariat cannot be taught to be emancipated, nor can it be forced to be free. It has to be free for its liberation so that it is able to become free. Sustained mass demonstrations and social struggles, and therewith the politicisation of social labour relations, are the laboratory of the society of the 'free and equal'.

Idealism is the true realism

Those to whom human emancipation has meaning should not dread to be called idealists. They are. Idealism is the true reality of the spectre of communism. Reason without imagination creates monsters. Imagination without reason creates useless things. Reason wedded with imagination creates the beauty of communist struggle: 'all emancipation is a return of the human world and human relationships to humans themselves. Political emancipation is the reduction of man, on the one hand, to a member of bourgeois society, an egoistic and independent individual, on the other hand, to a citizen of the state, a moral person. Not until the real individual man has taken the abstract citizen back into himself and, as an individual man, has become a species-being in his empirical life, in his individual work and individual relationships, not until man recognises and organises his "forces propres" as social forces and thus no longer separates social forces from himself in the form of political forces, not until then will human emancipation be completed.'[40] This, then, is the conception of communism as social autonomy where nothing exists independently from the social individual, where the associated producers are in control of their own social forces. Social autonomy is not some sort of distant future. It is at issue in every struggle over the capitalist reduction to human purposes to some abstract labour, to cash and product. It is the means towards its end. In his introduction to his critique of Hegel's Philosophy of Law, Marx formulated the categorical imperative of human emancipation when he argued that all relations have to be abolished in which Man is a degraded, exploited, debased, forsaken and enslaved being'.[41] Communism is the practical movement of this imperative in and against bourgeois society. At times this movement is clearly visible to everybody who wants to see, at other times it is visible only to those who dare to see it.

Postscript

Human emancipation, communism, is not a condition that needs to be created in some future society. It is the real negation of existing conditions from within these conditions themselves. The communist individual is someone who lives the communist imperative in everyday life, from mundane routines to the most refined expressions. The communist individual is someone who understands the practical meaning of the struggle for a society in which the 'free development of each is the condition of the free development of all'. The communist individual cannot be derived from hypothesised, objective conditions and structures. The communist individual has no price. The community of communist individuals does not derive from capitalism. It does not compete with capitalism. It struggles against it. Nor is this community a mere idealist hypothesis. Its reality is neither given nor assumed. Its reality is its own reality. Nothing is as it seems. There is no certainty.

NOTES

1. Cf. Karl Marx, *Capital*, Vol. I, Lawrence & Wishart, London, 1983, p. 85.

2. Karl Marx, *Capital*, op. cit., p. 447.
3. Karl Marx, *Capital*, Vol. III, Lawrence & Wishart, London, 1966, p. 818. On class as a negative concept, see Werner Bonefeld ''Capital, Labour and Primitive Accumulation. On Class and Constitution', in Dinerstein, A.C. and M. Neary (eds.), *The Labour Debate*, Ashgate, Aldershot.
4. Karl Marx, *Capital*, Vol. I, op. cit, p. 707. On the permanence of primitive accumulation and associated forms of exploitation, see, for example, Mariarosa Dalla Costa, 'Capitalism and Reproduction', and Midnight Notes, 'The New Enclosures', both in Werner Bonefeld (Hersg), *Imagining the Future—Subverting the Present*, Autonomedia, New York, 2008.
5. See Simon Clarke, *Marx, Marginalism and Modern Social Theory*, second edition, Palgrave, London, 1992, for an account of Adam Smith's conception of class and modern sociology, including one has to add, its analytical and structuralist Marxist off-springs. See Werner Bonefeld, 'Capital, Labour and Primitive Accumulation', in Ana Dinerstein and Mike Neary (Hersg), *The Labour Debate*, Ashgate, Aldershot, 1992.
6. See Karl Marx, *Capital*, Vol. I, op. cit., p. 559.
7. Karl Marx, *Capital*, Vol. I, op. cit., p. 546.
8. See Hans-Jürgen Krahl, *Vom Ende der abstrakten Arbeit*, Materialis MP 23, Materialis Verlag, Frankfurt, 1984, pp. 115-16. 'Objective possibility' is of course a Weberian term: objects have no possibilities, subjects do. Objective possibilities are a product of social relations, and possess their validity only for and within these relations. The human subject objectifies herself in the object, however perverted (verrückt) this object might be in the form of capital.
9. Wolfgang Fritz Haug, *Vorlesungen zur Einführung ins 'Kapital'*, 6th Ausgabe, Argument Verlag, Hamburg, 2005, p. 11.
10. Karl Marx/Friedrich Engels, *Die heilige Familie*, MEW 2, Dietz, Berlin, 1980, p. 98.
11. Karl Marx, *Grundrisse*, Penguin, London, 1973, p. 105.
12. In the 1980s, Ernest Mandel illustrated this dissociation by speaking about an upside down pyramid, in which an ever-increasing credit-superstructure is supported by a receding base-productive accumulation. This upside down pyramid presents a huge, potentially irredeemable mortgage on the future exploitation of labour. The 'golden age' of post-war capitalism is now a memory, as is the blood-letting through war and gas. What the resolution to irredeemable debt can mean, stands

behind us as a warning of a possibly nightmarish future. See Ernest Mandel *Die Krise*, Konkret, Hamburg, 1987. I have analysed this development in *The Recomposition of the British State During the 1980s*, Dartmouth, Aldershot, 1993, and updated in 'Human Progress and Capitalist Development', in Andreas Bieler et al., *Global Restructuring, State, Capital and Labour*, Palgrave, London, 2006. The argument on the radicality of the challenge draws on Ricardo Bellofiore, 'Lavori in Corso', *Common Sense*, 22, 1997.

13. Joachim Hirsch, 'The State Apparatus and Social Reproduction', in Holloway, J. and S. Picciotto (eds.) *State and Capital*, Arnold, London, p. 75, emphasis added.
14. See Joachim Hirsch/Roland Roth, *Das neue Gesicht des Kapitalismus*, VSA, Hamburg, 1986, p. 37.
15. It would be unfair to attribute this point to Hirsch. It belongs to the second and third Internationals, and the structuralist traditions, most prominently Althusser, upon whom Hirsch draws. See Alfred Schmidt, *History and Structure*, MIT Press, Cambridge, MA, 1983, for a critique of structuralist theories of history. See John Holloway *Change the World without Taking Power*, Pluto, London, 2nd ed. 2005, for an account on the making of history.
16. Louis Althusser, 'Averstissement aux lecteurs du Capital', Preface to the paperback edition of *Le Capital I*, Paris, ed. Sociales, 1969, p. 7.
17. Marx's mockery is as topical now as it was then: 'what divides these gentlemen from the bourgeois apologist is, on the one side, their sensitivity to the contradictions included in the system; on the other, the utopian inability to grasp the necessary difference between the real and the ideal form of bourgeois society, which is the cause of their desire to undertake the superfluous business of realising the ideal expression again, which is in fact only the inverted projection [*Lichtbild*] of this reality' (Marx, *Grundrisse*, op. cit., 1973, pp. 248-49). Communism does not derive from capitalism. Nor does it compete with capitalism. It is an alternative to capitalism. On this see Nick Dyer-Witheford, *Cyber-Marx*, University of Illinois Press, Chicago, 1999. See also Simon Clarke, *Marx, Marginalism and Modern Sociology*, Palgrave, London, 2nd ed. 1992. Clarke argues that orthodox Marxism derives its concepts and analysis from classical political economy, bypassing Marx's critique of political economy.
18. Karl Marx, *Grundrisse*, op. cit., p. 87.

19. Karl Marx, *Zur Kritik der Politischen Ökonomie*, in MEW 13, Dietz, Berlin, 1981, p. 8.
20. Johannes Agnoli, *Subversive Theorie. "Die Sache selbst" und ihre Geschichte*, Ça ira, Freiburg, 1996, p. 29.
21. Antonio Negri, *Marx Beyond Marx: Lessons on the Grundrisse*, Bergin and Garvey, Massachusetts, 1984, p. 72.
22. 'In fact, the realm of freedom actually begins only where labour which is determined by necessity and mundane considerations ceases; thus in the very nature of things it lies beyond the sphere of actual material production...Freedom in this field can only consist in socialised Man [*Mensch*], the associated producers, rationally regulating their interchange with Nature, bringing it under their common control, instead of being ruled by the blind forces of nature...But it nonetheless still remains a realm of necessity. Beyond it begins that development of human energy which is an end in itself, the true realm of freedom, which, however, can blossom forth only with this realm of necessity as its basis'. Karl Marx, *Capital*, Vol. III, op. cit., p. 820. See the exchange between Wildcat and John Holloway for an assessment. Wildcat and John Holloway, 'Wildcat (Germany) reads John Holloway—A Debate on Marxism and the Politics of Dignity', *Common Sense*, No. 24, 1999.
23. Karl Marx, *Capital*, Vol. I, op. cit., p. 53. See Simon Clarke, *Marx's Theory of Crisis*, Palgrave, London, 1993, for a succinct treatment of this point.
24. Ferruccio Gambino, 'A Critique of the Fordism of the Regulation School', in Werner Bonefeld (Hersg.), *Revolutionary Writing*, Autonomedia, New York, 2003, p. 104. The social calamity of capitalist development is taken from Karl Marx, *Capital*, Vol. I, op. cit., p. 416.
25. As the father of modern utilitarianism, Jeremy Bentham, put it when recommending that children be made to work at the age of four rather than fourteen: 'Ten precious years in which nothing is done! Nothing for industry! Nothing for improvement, moral or intellectual!' Quoted in Michael Perelman, *The Invention of Capitalism*, Duke University Press, Durham and London, 2000, p. 22.
26. Louis Althusser, *For Marx*, trans. B. Brewster, Verso, London, 1996. Nicos Poulantzas, 'Theorie und Geschichte. Kurze Bemerkung über den Gegenstand des "Kapitals"', in Walter Euchner/Alfred Schmidt (Hersg.) *Kritik der politischen Ökonomie. 100 Jahre Kapital*, EVA, Frankfurt, 1968.

27. See Beverley Silver, *Forces of Labour*, Cambridge University Press, Cambridge, 2003. Wildcat, *Unruhen in China*, Beilage der Wildcat No. 80, December 2007. John Holloway, 'Zapata in Wallstreet', in Werner Bonefeld / Kosmas Psychopedis (Hersg.) *The Politics of Change*, Palgrave, London, 2000; and Werner Bonefeld/John Holloway 'Money and Class Struggle', in ibid. (ed.) *Global Capital, National State and the Politics of Money*, Palgrave, London, 1996.
28. Georg Lukács, *History and Class Consciousness*, Merlin, London, 1970, p. 172. Ernst Bloch, *Logos der Materie*, Suhrkamp, Frankfurt, 2000. Oskar Negt/Alexander Kluge, *Public Sphere and Experience*, University of Minnesota Press, Minneapolis, 1993. Michael Hardt/Antonio Negri, *Multitude: War and Democracy in the Age of Empire*, Penguin, London, 2004. Negri's biologised subject complements Althusser's naturalised objectivity. On this, see my 'Human Practice and Perversion: Beyond Autonomy and Structure', in Werner Bonefeld (Hersg.), *Revolutionary Writing*, op. cit.
29. Gabriel Garcia Marquez, Newspaper Interview, *El Nuevo Diario*, Managua, April 25, 1990.
30. See Michel Löwy, 'Dialectica de civilizacion: barbarie y modernidad en el siglo XX', *Herramienta*, No. 22, 2003. For a conceptualization of the means and ends of human emancipation, see the collection of essays published in Werner Bonefeld/Sergio Tischler (Hersg) *What is to be Done? Leninism, Anti-Leninist Marxism and the Question of Revolution Today*, Ashgate, Aldershot, 2002. For an account on the fate of workers' self-organisation in the immediate aftermath of the Russian Revolution, see Simon Pirani, *The Russian Revolution in Retreat*, Routledge, London, 2008. See Ana Dinerstein 'Lessons from a Journey: The Piquetero Movement in Argentina', in Werner Bonefeld, *Subversion...*, op. cit., on the incorporation of the majority of the Piqueteros into the state under the first Kirchner administration.
31. Karl Marx/Friedrich Engels, *The Communist Manifesto*, Pluto, London, 1996, p. 28.
32. Karl Marx, *Capital*, Vol. I, op. cit., p. 233.
33. See footnote 27.
34. Karl Marx/Friedrich Engels, *The Communist Manifesto*, op. cit., pp. 18-19.
35. 'Die Freiheit ist ein leerer Wahn, solange eine Menschenklasse die andere ungestraft aushungern kann. Die Gleichheit ist ein leerer Wahn, solange der Reiche mit dem Monopol das Recht

über Leben und Tod seiner Mitmenschen ausübt'. Jacques Roux, 'Das "Manifest der Enragés"', in Jacques Roux, *Freiheit wird die Welt erobern, Reden und Schriften*, Röderberg, Frankfurt/a.m., 1985, p. 147. Roux belonged to the Enragés, the Reds of the French Revolution.

36. Enlarging on Agnoli's argument on subversion (Thesis IV), Man objects to be treated as a mere economic resource.
37. Karl Marx, *Die deutsche Ideologie*, op. cit, p. 26.
38. Walter Benjamin, 'Geschichtsphilosphische Thesen' in *Zur Kritik der Gewalt und andere Aufsätze* Suhrkamp, Franfkurt, 1965, p. 84.
39. Simon Clarke, 'Class Struggle and the Global Overaccumulation of Capital', in Robert Albritton et al. (Hersg.), *Phases of Capitalist Development*, Palgrave, London, 2001, pp. 90-91.
40. Karl Marx, *Zur Judenfrage*, in MEW 1, Dietz, Berlin, 1964, p. 370.
41. Karl Marx, *Zur Kritik der Hegelschen Rechtsphilosophie. Einleitung*, I MEW 1, Dietz, Berlin, 1956, p. 385.

3

Notes on Fetishism, History and Uncertainty: Beyond the Critique of Austerity

> 'What divides these gentlemen [the French socialists] from the bourgeois apologist is, on the one side, their sensitivity to the contradictions included in the system; on the other, the utopian inability to grasp the necessary difference between the real and the ideal form of bourgeois society, which is the cause of their desire to undertake the superfluous business of realising the ideal expression again, which is in fact only the inverted projection [*Lichtbild*] of this reality' (Marx, 1973, pp. 248-49).

Preface

We live at a time that resounds with misery. The headlines have changed from war and terror to what seems like a never-ending global economic crisis. Against the background of debt, default and sluggish rates of economic growth at best, accumulation by dispossession is back en vogue, a whole generation of workers appears redundant, and a whole mass of people have been cut off from the means of subsistence, struggling to survive —and despite appearances to the contrary, war and terror continue unabated. In this context, the notion that capitalism produces deplorable situations is a most optimistic point of view. Deplorable conditions (*Zustände*) are not the same as deplorable situations (*Mißstände)*. The one says that poverty is a capitalist condition. Challenging it requires a fundamental change in the social relations of production. On the other hand, deplorable situations describe entirely avoidable socio-economic circumstances, be they the result of a chance development, government incompetence, or hard-nosed class-politics. As such it can be rectified by well-meaning political interventions and political programmes that benefit society at large.[1] Instead of capitalist profit, miserable situations require resolution by political means that hold the economy accountable to the democratic aspirations for a freedom from want. Deplorable situations require thus a social activism that challenges This misery and That outrage, seeking to alleviate and rectify This and That. What however are the social preconditions that constitute the necessity of This poverty and That misery? After all, what is needed is a praxis that fights the underlying conditions of misery. Adorno (1972) therefore condemns activism for its own sake, and rejects it as a pseudo-praxis that fights this and that but leaves the conditions that render this and that entirely untouched. In this way, 'activism' is not only affirmative of existing society but also regressive—it deludes itself that however bad the situation, it can be rectified by this or that policy, by this or that technical means. The activism of the given situation feels the pain of the world and offers its own programme as the means of salvation. The activism against this or that is delusional in its conception of society. It deceives those whose interests it pretends to represent by making them believe that a resolution to their plight is really just a matter of proper government. In its essence, activism for this cause or that cause is a political advertisement for some alternative party of government. It transforms the protest against a really existing misery that blights the life of a whole class of individuals into a selling point for political gain.

On society and economic nature

Critical thought is none other than the cunning of reason when confronted with a social reality in which the poor and miserable are required to subsidise the financial system for the sake of sustaining the illusion of fictitious wealth. Yet, this subsidy is entirely necessary in existing society, to prevent its implosion.

This rational irrationality of a capitalistically organised mode of social reproduction is at the centre of the critique of political economy. Its critique is subversive. It asks why human social reproduction takes this irrational form. Subversion focuses on human conditions and focuses on essentials: 'Free labour contains the pauper' (Marx, 1973, p. 604) and capitalist wealth entails the poverty of dispossessed labour in its conception.Its focus on essentials entails intransigence towards the existent patterns of the world. It demands that all relations 'in which man is a debased, enslaved, forsaken, despicable being have to be overthrown' (Marx, 1975, p. 182). Debasement subsists as society unaware of itself; a society that is, in which human sensuous practice exists, say, in the form of a movement of coins that impose themselves with seemingly irresistible force on the acting subjects as if the world of coins were a world apart. The fetishism of commodities makes the human world appear as one that is governed by natural, immutable economic laws. Yet, nature has nothing to do with it. What appears as an objective force of economic nature is and remains a socially constituted force. Society is governed by economic abstractions that appear as forces of nature. Economic nature is a socially constituted nature. Society asserts itself in the form of a relationship between things and thus exists in and through the movement of socially constituted things.

Society is 'objective' insofar as and 'because' its 'own subjectivity is not transparent'. Society is subjective 'in that it refers back to human beings which form it' (Adorno, 1993a, p. 43). Objectivity 'realises itself only through individuals'. Society as a mere object comprises the socially necessary delusion that the social structures and social laws are innately natural. 'The thesis that society is subject to natural laws is ideology' (Adorno, 1973, p. 355). Social objectivity does not posit itself—it is 'the posited universal of the social individuals that constitute it' (1993b, p. 127). What this means is well brought out by Marx (1973, p. 239) when he writes in the money fetish that 'a social relation, a definite relation between individuals ... appears as a metal, a stone, as a purely physical external thing which can be found, as such, in nature, and which is indistinguishable in form from its natural existence' That is, social objectivity 'does not lead a life of its own' (Adorno, 1993b, p. 127). It is a socially constituted objectivity—social relations vanish in their appearance as a metal or a stone, and this appearance is real. There is only one world, and that is the world of appearance. What appears in the appearance of society as a 'stone', or a 'coin', is however a definite social relationship between individuals subsisting as a relationship between 'coins'. Society appears as some transcendental thing that governs by means of the 'invisible hand', which takes 'care of both the beggar and the king' (Adorno, 1973, p. 251). Its transcend character is real: Money makes the world go round; yet, it does so only because, in capitalism, the social individuals are governed by the product of their own hand. In short, the world does indeed manifest itself behind the backs of acting individuals and society is indeed governed by real abstractions; yet, it is their own world (cf. Marcuse, 1988, p. 151).

Marx's critique of fetishism amounts thus to a judgement on existence. That is, the critique of political economy amounts to a conceptualised praxis (*begriffenden Praxis*) of definite social relations in their appearance as relations, say, between coins (Schmidt, 1974, p. 207). It holds that theoretical mysteries find their rational explanation in human practice and in the comprehension of this practice, and argues that this practice exists against itself in the form of relations of economic objectivity.The limit to reification is reified Man, and in the face of reified Man, the critique of fetishism is an attempt at making society conscious of its own 'monstrous' world. In short, the meaning of objectivity excludes the possibility that it can also be a subject. However, to be an object is part of the meaning of subjectivity. Subjectivity means objectification. In its capitalist form it appears in the logic of things. Appearance [*Schein*] "is the enchantment of the subject in its own world" (Adorno 1969: 159). The circumstance that objectification [*Gegenständlichkeit*] exists in the form of a relationship between coins does thus not imply that there is an as yet undiscovered, and indeed undiscoverable, logic that lies solely within the thing itself. Only as a socially determinate object can the object be an object (see

Adorno 1969: 157). Reason exists—but in irrational form. The irrational world is a rational world.

Marx's work focuses on forms, at first on forms of consciousness (i.e. religion and law), then later on the forms of political economy. This focus on forms entails a critique of social relations that subsist in an inverted form of society—one that is governed not by the social individuals themselves but, rather, one that is governed by 'product' of their own hand. That is to say, every social 'form', even the most simple form like, for example, the commodity, 'is already an inversion and causes relations between people to appear as attributes of things' (Marx, 1972, p. 508) or, more emphatically, each form is a 'perverted form' (Marx, 1979, p. 90).[2] The critique of economic categories as perverted social forms subverts the economic idea of cash, price and profit by revealing their social constitution. The movement of 'coins' does not express some abstractly conceived economic matter. It expresses a definite social relationship between individuals subsisting as a relationship between things and coins. In capitalism individuals are really governed by the movement of coins—they carry their relationship with society, and therewith their access to the means of subsistence, in their pockets. Although coins tend to inflate or become depressed, they are not subjects. Yet, they impose themselves on, and also in and though, the person to the point of madness and disaster, from the socially necessary consciousness of cash and product, money and profit, to poverty and famine, and bloodshed and war. The bourgeois concepiton of wealth is money as more money, and this idea of more money objectifies itself in the persons as mere 'agents of value' (Adorno, 173, p. 311) who depend for their life on the manner in which the 'logic of economic things' unfolds—access to the means of subsistence appears to be governed by fate and fate appears in the form of economic growth, which if money does not posit itself as more money cuts off a whole class of people from the means of subsistence. What a monstrosity! An economic thing, this coin, that in its nature really is nothing more than a piece of metal manifests itself as a power by which 'the life of all men hangs by' (Adorno, 1973, p. 320). However, this is not a monstrosity of economic nature nor is it one of reified things. That is, the mythological idea of fate becomes no less mythical when it is demythologised "into a secular 'logic of things'" (ibid., p. 319) or into an abstract system-logic that structures the economic behaviours by means of price signals, which comprises the freedom to wealth and the freedom to starve. Its economic nature is in its entirety a socially constituted nature.

On society and praxis

There is, says Adorno, a need for a 'practice that fights barbarism', and yet, he argues rightly, there can be no such practice (Adorno, 1962, p. 30). Barbarism cannot be fought in a direct and immediate manner—what really does it mean to struggle against money, resist the movement of coins, combat the law of value, and fight poverty in a society that contains poverty in its concept of wealth? A 'practice that fights barbarism' is about the social preconditions that render barbarism. To put this point in an entirely different manner:The struggle for humanisation points the struggle against constituted relations of misery in the right direction; the humanisation of social relations is the purpose and end of the struggle for the human emancipation from reified economic relations, from relations in which an increase in social wealth manifests itself to the class that is tied to work in the form of a constant struggle for access to the means of subsistence. However, the effort of humanising inhuman conditions is confronted by the paradox that it presupposes as eternal those same inhuman conditions that provoke the effort of humanisation in the first place. Inhuman conditions are not just an impediment to humanisation but a premise of its concept. What then does it mean to say 'no'?

It is not the independence of economic categories of cash and coin, value and money, as forces over and above, and also in and through, the social individuals that require explanation. Rather, what requires explanation is the social relations of production that manifest themselves as a relationship between economic things, which assert themselves behind the backs of those same individuals that comprise and sustain society.

Adorno's notion that the 'total movement of society' is 'antagonistic from the outset' (Adorno, 1970, p. 304) entails therefore more than it first seems. Not only does the fetishism of commodities presuppose antagonistic social relations but society exists also by virtue of the class antagonism. That is to say, 'society stays alive, not despite its antagonism, but by means of it' (Adorno, 1973, p. 320). The struggle against capitalism is therefore not a struggle for the working class. Whichever way one looks at it, to be a member of the working class is a great 'misfortune' (Marx, 1983, p. 477). That is so say, class is not a positive category. It is a critical concept of the false society. The critique of class society finds its positive resolution not in better paid workers or conditions of full-employment, etc. It finds its positive resolution only in the classless society, in which mankind has rid itself of 'all the muck of ages and found itself anew' (Marx and Engels 1976: 53)—as a commune of 'communist individuals' (Marcuse 1958: 127).

In a world governed by the movement of coins, the critique of class society is entirely negative. A constructive critique of class society does not amount to a critical practice. It amounts, argue Horkheimer and Adorno (1972) and Adorno (1970), to 'ticket thinking'. Such thinking is 'one-dimensional'. It argues in interests of the wage labourer with a claim to power. That is, rather than understanding capital as a social relationship, it takes capital to be an economic thing that given the right balance of class forces, can be made to work for the benefit of workers. Ticket thinking proclaims 'falseness' (Adorno 2008a: 28). Instead of the 'optimism of the left' that puts forth a programme of capitalist transformation which does 'not talk about the devil but looks on the bright side' (Adorno 1978: 114), there is therefore need to understand the capitalist conceptuality of social labour.

Affirmative conceptions of class, however well-meaning and benevolent in their intentions, presuppose the working class as productive force that deserves a better, a new deal. What is a fair wage? Marx made the point that '"price of labour" is just as irrational as a yellow logarithm' (Marx, 1966, p. 818). The demand for fair wages and fair labour conditions abstracts from the very conditions of 'fairness' in capitalism, which is founded on the divorce of social labour from the means of subsistence, and instead of overcoming this divorce which is the foundation of capital and labour, it proclaims that dispossessed workers be paid better. That is, the divorce of social labour from the means of subsistence transforms labour into a proletarian who is 'the slave of other individuals who have made themselves the owners of the means of human existence' (Marx, 1970, p. 13, translation amended). Why does this content, that is, human social reproduction, take the form of an equivalent exchange between the owners of the means of subsistence and the dispossessed seller of labour power, and how can it be that wealth expands by means of an exchange between equivalent values? The seller of labour power is fundamentally a human factor of surplus labour-time, which is the foundation of surplus value and thus profit. The equivalence of an exchange between quantitatively different values has thus to do with the transformation of labour into a surplus value producing labour activity which expands social wealth, allowing money to lay golden eggs. Even on the assumption that when hiring labour, equivalent is exchanged for equivalent, this transaction between the seller and buyer of labour 'is all that only the old dodge of every conqueror who buys commodities from the conquered with the money he has robbed them of' (1983, p. 456). That is to say, theory on behalf of the working class affirms the existence of a class of people tied to surplus value production. Chapter 48 of Volume Three of *Capital* provides Marx's critique of the theory of class proposed by classical political economy (and shared by modern social science), according to which class interests are determined by the revenue sources (or, in Weberian terms, market situation) of social groups, rather than being founded in the social relations of production as Marx argues (on this see Clarke, 1992). Political Economy is indeed a scholarly dispute how the booty pumped out of the labourer may be divided and distributed amongst the component classes of society (Marx, 1983, p. 559)—and clearly, the more the labourer gets, the better. After all, it is her social labour that produces the 'wealth of nations'.

However, the critique of political economy is not political economy. In distinction to political economy's focus on the distribution of wealth, it asks about the conceptuality of social wealth, that is wealth in the form of value, and it asks how this wealth if produced, by whom, and for what purpose. According to Marx, wealth is produced by labour for the sake of greater wealth in the form of value, and value isvalue in exchange that becomes visible in the form of money. Value is wealth as valorised value. Time is money. The critique of political amounts thus to a conceptualised practice of capitalist form of social wealth as one that is founded on the transformation of the workers' life-time into labour-time. There is no time to waste and there is always more time to catch. This, then, is the 'nibbling and cribbling at meal times' as 'moments are the elements of profit' (Marx, 1983, pp. 232-33). The time of value is the time of socially necessary labour-time. Work that is not completed within this time is wasted, valueless, regardless of the labour-time that went into it, the sweat and tears of its productive efforts, the usefulness of the material wealth that was created, and the needs that it could satisfy. From the appropriation of unpaid labour-time to the endless struggle over the division between necessary labour-time and surplus labour-time, from the 'imposition' of labour-time by time-theft, this 'petty pilferings of minutes', 'snatching a few minutes' (ibid., p. 232), to the stealing from the worker of atoms of additional unpaid labour time by means of great labour flexibility and 'systematic robbery of what is necessary for the life of the workman' (Marx, 1983, p. 402), the life-time of the worker is labour-time. The worker then appears as 'nothing more than personified labour-time' (Marx, 1983, p. 233)—a *'time's carcase'* (on this, see Bonefeld, 2010b).

The notion, then, that the hell of a class-ridden society can be reformed for the sake of workers is regressive in that it projects a 'conformist rebellion' (Horkheimer 1985), that, say, instead of ending slavery, seeks a new deal for slaves. Although 'the world contains opportunities enough for success [communism] ...everything is bewitched' (Adorno and Horkheimer 2011: 20).That is, there is only one social reality, and this is the reality of the 'enchanted and perverted' world of capital (Marx 1966: 830), which reproduces itself not despite the class struggle but rather by virtue of it. Sensuous human activity subsists through the world of economic things, and thus appears 'as a thing' (Marx 1973, p. 157).

In capitalism, every progress turns into a calamity

Capitalist social relations have produced a staggering expansion in social wealth and phenomenal increase in labour productivity. Within a miniscule historical period of time, it has transformed human society beyond recognition. Nevertheless, despite this unprecedented expansion of human productive power, the time of labour has not diminished. In capitalism, every social progress turns into a calamity. Every increase in labour productivity shortens the hours of labour but in its capitalist form, it lengthens them. The introduction of sophisticated machinery lightens labour but in its capitalist form, it heightens the intensity of labour. Every increase in the productivity of labour increases the material wealth of the producers but in its capitalist form makes them paupers. Most importantly of all, greater labour productivity sets labour free, makes labour redundant. But rather then shortening the hours of work and thus absorbing all labour into production on the basis of a shorter working day, freeing life-time from the 'realm of necessity', those in employment are exploited more intensively, while those made redundant find themselves on the scrap heap of a mode of production that sacrifices '"human machines" on the pyramids of accumulation' (Gambino, 2003, p. 104).[3]

Capitalist wealth is wealth in value. Value is category of constant expansion, on the pain of ruin and by means of ruin. Value is wealth in the form of restless expansion of abstract wealth *qua* destruction. Concealed in the concept of capital as self-valorising value lies the conceptuality of social labour. The necessity of its affirmation *qua* destruction—discussed by Marx at times as the dialectic between the forces and the relations of production—belongs to the constituted existence of social labour in the form of capital.

Destruction is the constituted nightmare of the capitalist mode of social reproduction:

> Society suddenly finds itself put back into a state of momentary barbarism; it appears as if famine, a universal war of devastation had cut off the supply of every means of subsistence; industry and commerce seem to be destroyed; and why? Because there is too much civilisation, too much means of subsistence; too much industry, too much commerce. The productive forces at the disposal of society no longer tend to further the development of the conditions of bourgeois property; on the contrary, they have become too powerful for these conditions, by which they are fettered, and as soon as they overcome these fetters, they bring disorder into the whole of bourgeois society, endanger the existence of bourgeois property. The conditions of bourgeois society are too narrow to comprise the wealth created by them. And how does bourgeois society get over these crises? On the one hand by enforced destruction of a mass of productive forces; on the other, by the conquest of new markets, and by the more thorough exploitation of the old ones. (Marx and Engels 1996: 18–19)

This commentary on globalisation by the 29-year-old Marx is not a brilliant anticipation, which after all turned out to be far too optimistic. Rather, it conceptualises the critical subject and, in doing so, shows what lies within it. What lies within the concept of capitalist wealth are its determinate necessities. These belong to the critical subject of society unaware of itself and constitute its conceptuality. Creation *qua* destruction is a valid necessity of capitalist social relations—it belongs to its conceptuality [*Begrifflichkeit*]. "Conceptuality expresses the fact that, no matter how much blame may attach to the subject's contribution, the conceived world is not its own but a world hostile to the subject" (Adorno 1973: 167). Man vanishes in her own world and exists against herself as a personification of economic categories—an "alienated subject" (see Backhaus 1992) that constitutes the world of things and is invisible, lost and denied in its own world—the expansion of wealth entails the disappearance of wealth as a whole class of people tied to work is cut off from the means of subsistence as if the social metabolism really is governed by the mythical idea of fate.

There is only one human measure that cannot be modified. It can only be lost (Max Frisch)

Marx conceives of communism as the real movement of the working class (Marx and Engels 1976) and argues that history is a history of class struggle (Marx and Engels 1996). This argument recognises that history has been a history of rulers and ruled, and this is the only history that has been—a bad—universality of transition from one mode of domination to another. The universality of history is, however, both real and false. In the history of the victors the victims of history are invisible, and it is their invisibility that makes history appear as a universal history that akin to a sequence of events, records the times of glorious rule, from which the memory of struggle and insubordination is necessarily expunged. The courage, cunning, and suffering of the dead disappears twice, once in a defeat in which 'even the dead will not be safe' from an enemy that 'has not ceased to be victorious' (Benjamin 1999: 247), and then again in the present, which either denies that the dead ever existed or ritualises their struggles as an heroic act that culminated in the present as the unrivalled manifestation of their bravery (Tischler, 2005). The struggles of the past transform into a monument of history, erected in celebration of the present mode of domination, for which the dead perform the role of legitimising fodder. It is true, says Benjamin, that 'all the rulers are the heirs of those who conquered before them'. There is thus no 'document of civilisation' that is 'not at the same time a document of barbarism' (Benjamin 1999: 248). History though universal in its appearance, is not some automatic thing that unfolds on behalf of the masters of the world by force of its own objectively unfolding victorious logic. 'Whoever has emerged victorious participates to this day in the triumphal procession, in which the present rulers step over those who are lying prostrate' (Benjamin 1999: 248). Nevertheless, however universal the progress of history might appear, the future has not already been written, class struggles have to be fought, and their outcomes are uncertain, unpredictable, and fundamentally open, then and now. What appears linear to us was contested, uncertain and unpredictable at its own time. Its progress towards the present appears logical in its directional dynamic because the time of the present eliminates any doubt in its own historical veracity as a pre-determined outcome of a sequence of recorded events that dated the time of the present in the past.

What alternatives might there have been in the past and how many struggles have been at the knife's edge and could have led to a course of history that would be unrecognisable to us? There is no inevitability in history, nor is history an irresistible force. It is made by the acting subjects themselves and what is made by Man can be changed by Man. History appears inevitable and irresistible only afterwards, which gives history the appearance of some objective force and directional dynamic, a telos of becoming and achievement, towards which it seemingly strives. For the proponents of present society, history has been concluded. Others say that it is still continuing towards some assumed socialist or communist destiny, at which point it will conclude. History does however not make history. That is to say, '[h]istory does nothing, does not "possess vast wealth", does not "fight battles"! It is Man, rather, the real, living Man who does all that, who does possess and fight, it is not "history" that uses Man [*Mensch*] as a means to pursue its ends, as if it were a person apart. History is nothing but the activity of Man pursuing its ends' (Marx 1980: 98). Historical materialism is not the dogma indicated by clever opponents and unthinking proponents alike, but a critique of things understood dogmatically. That is to say, the 'human anatomy contains a key to the anatomy of the ape', but not conversely, the anatomy of the ape does not explain the anatomy of Man (Marx 1973: 105). If the anatomy of the ape would really explain the anatomy of Man than the ape would already possess Man as the innate necessity of its evolution—a natural teleology or an already written future.[4] The future, however, has not already been written. Nor will it be the result of some abstractly conceived objective logic of historical development. History does not unfold, as if it were a person apart. History has to be made, and will be made, by Man pursuing her ends. These ends themselves are not theologically determined, naturally founded, or historically active. The purpose of capitalism is the profitable accumulation of abstract wealth. The commune of human purpose is not an existing human purpose. Its reality is a negative one. That is to say, linear conceptions of history do not reveal abstract historical laws. They reveal accommodation of thought and practice to the existing 'objective conditions'. Linear conceptions of history conceive of it as a continuum of progress of the present into its own future.

The political left claims thathistory is on the side of the oppressed and thatthe struggle of the oppressed therefore moving with the current of history's forward march. This proclamation of progress makes 'dogmatic claims' (Benjamin 1999: 252) about a future of freed proletarians. How might one conceive of a liberated future that is not also a future present? Benjamin calls the conception of history that conceives of existing reality as transition towards communism, the 'bordello' (ibid.: 253) of historical thought. It criticises capitalism with a claim to power, envisages progress as a matter of party political success, advertises itself as the theory and practice of progress of a history that 'runs its course...according to its own dialectic' (Lukacs, in Pinkus 1975: 74). At its best this idea of history as imminent progress represents the sentimentality of the epoch, at worst it believes in itself, asserting a dogmatic claim to power for the sake of power.

On the critique of progress

History has no independent reality. It appears as a sequence of events, from one battle to another and from this division of labour to that division of labour. This appearance is real but by itself, devoid of meaning. What does it really mean to say that history is a sequence of events? Events of what and what was so eventful? Its appearance as an objectively unfolding force towards the present conceptuality of social wealth is deceptive. It gives raise to the idea of the coming of the society of human purposes as an 'event' of historical becoming towards which history somewhat strives. This view of history makes it appear as if the society of the free and equal derives from existing society, demeaning the very idea the society of human purposes. The difficulty of conceiving of such a society independently from capitalism, has to do with its very idea. In distinction to the pursuit of profit, seizure of the state, pursuit and preservation of political power, and economic value and human resource, it follows a completely different entelechy of human development —on in which wealth is free time, the purpose of humanity it own purpose, and one in which equality is an equality of individuals human needs. For the sake of human emancipation, the idea of history as a force of relentless progress has to be abandoned—the idea of progress is tied to existing society, which legitimises the existence of poverty as a condition of future wealth.History appears as a transcendent force of progress only when one abstracts from it, leading to its description of a sequence of historical events, for which the terms 'histoıicity' provides the name. That is to say, in order to comprehend history, one needs to 'crack the continuum of history.'[5] One needs thus to think out of history, out of the battles, out of the struggles of the Levellers and Diggers, slave insurrections, peasant revolts, the struggles of Les Enragés, working class strikes, riots, insurrections, and revolutions, including St. Petersburg (1917) and Kronstadt (1921), and Barcelona (1936)[6], to appreciate the traditions of the oppressed, recognise the smell of danger and the stench of death, gain a sense of the courage and cunning of struggle, grasp the spirit of sacrifice, comprehend however fleetingly the density of a time at which history almost came to a standstill.[7] History does not lead anywhere; it has no telos, no objectives, no purpose, and it does not take sides. At its worst, it continuous on the path of victorious progress under darkened clouds and smoke filled skies. History is made. At best, its progress will be stopped. Such history has not been made yet, though it has often been attempted. In our time, this attempt is called communism—this attempt at negation that seeks to rid the world of 'all the muck of ages'.

What is cannot be

The true picture of the past, says Benjamin (1999: 247) 'flits by'. When? How? It flits by 'at a moment of danger', at moments of courageous struggle when the time of the present appears to have come to a hold, a time at which everything seems possible, and where everything is up in the air, a time of great unpredictability and uncertainty, and thus a time at which the 'bloody grimace' (Adorno 1975: 43) of progress attains actual force in the experience of struggle. Thus the true picture of the past flits by at a time of greatest uncertainty, a time at which the certainty of tomorrow dissolves and at which the monuments of the past crack to reveal their hidden secret. This is the time of historical comprehension, in which the mass produced view of a glorious history transforms form a historicity of events into an experienced history of death and destruction, pillage and rape, enslavement and dispossession. This then is the time of intense uncertainty that reveals the bloody grimace of the past struggles, which up-to-now had hidden in the seemingly civilised forms of rule and power. This then is the time at which the dead victims of history step off the monument build by the state in its role as memory entrepreneur (see Tischler 2005). There is no redemption. There is only the realisation that history was not what it seemed, and there is a sudden understanding of the earlier sacrifice and deadly struggle. The experience of a time at a standstill is intoxicating, and full of danger. It is this experience that allows a glimpse of the past to take hold in the present, revealing a deadly certainty. That is, redemption is a matter of staying alive at a time when the certainty of tomorrow is no more: for 'even the dead will not be safe' if 'the enemy' wins (Benjamin 1999: 247).

The time of human emancipation is akin to pulling the emergency-break on a run-away train—here and now so that the continuum of history 'come[s] to a stop' (Benjamin 1999: 254). Another way of putting this is to say: the future present is both a present in transition towards its own future and a now-time that explodes this continuum of history. The time for pulling the emergency break is not tomorrow. It is now. Compared with the time of the present, Now-Time appears as a myth. The present is the time of seeming certainty and predictability. Now time says that now is the time of uncertainty. Now is the time to stop the forward march of the time of the clock, adding units of time to units of time, ticking and tacking according to the rhythm of a world in which time is money and money is wealth. Now-time appears as a myth because its acuity is a time that does not add to itself (Bonefeld 2010b). It does not move forward in relentless pursuit of abstract wealth, accumulating living labour on the pyramids of abstract wealth, appropriating additional atoms of unpaid labour time for the sake of an accumulation of abstract wealth alone. In Now-time, time is courage and cunning. Now is the time for taking aim 'at the clocks' so that their ticking and tacking stops, and time ceases to be money and instead becomes a time 'for enjoyment' (Marx, 1972, p. 252). Now-time is not the time of the present. It is a time against the present, seeking to stop it in its tracks. Conceived as a present time, now time ceases as a time that fights barbarism. Instead it converts the 'no' of Now-time into a 'conformist rebellion' for existing conditions, which it defends with doctrinaire belief in the progress of the present, according to which all will be well in the future once the communist bead of the rosary of history has slipped through our hands.[8]

Towards a conclusion without promise

Only a reified consciousness can declare that it is in possession of the requisite knowledge, political capacity, and technical expertise not only for resolving capitalist crises but, also, to do so in the interests of workers. Its world-view describes capitalist economy as an irrationally organised practice of labour, and proposes socialism as a rationally organised practice of labour by means of conscious planning by public authority. The anti-capitalism of central economic planning is abstract in its negation of the capitalistically organised mode of social reproduction. 'Abstract negativity' (Adorno 2008a: 25) barks in perpetuity and without bite. Instead, it sniffs out the miserable world, from the outside as it were, and puts itself forward as having the capacity, ability, insight, and means for resolving the crisis of capitalist economy 'for the workers' (see ibid.). Abstract negativity describes the theology of anti-capitalism. Theologically conceived, anti-capitalism is devoid of Now-Time. Instead of rupturing the continuum of history, it promises deliverance from misery amidst 'a pile of debris' that 'grows skyward' (Benjamin 1999: 249). Benjamin's thesis on the Angel of History says that the poor and miserable will not be liberated unless they liberate themselves, by their own effort, courage, and cunning.Herbert Marcuse focuses the conundrum of this argument most succinctly when he argues that the workers have to be free for their liberation so that they are able to become free (Marcuse 1964). In his view, workers can free themselves only insofar as they are not workers, on the basis of their non-identity. Marcuse's argument is to the point: to stop the progress of capitalism requires a non-capitalist identity, and the difficulty of its conception is a simple one: such an identity does not belong to the present, which is a capitalist present. What really does it mean to say 'no' to a capitalistically organised mode of human subsistence? To say 'no' to capitalism is simple. But to say what the 'no' is, is difficult. For one, the 'no' is not external to but operates within that same society which it opposes. Like Marx's summons of class struggle as the motor of history, the 'no' drives the negative world forward. It is its dynamic force. Furthermore, to say what the 'no' is compromises the 'no' insofar as it becomes positive in its affirmative yes to something that has no valid content except the very society that is opposes. The 'no' is immanent to bourgeois society and gives it its dynamic.

There is thus need for a realistic conception of the struggle for the society of human purposes. Class struggle has to be rediscovered as the laboratory of human emancipation. This struggle does not follow some abstract idea. It is a struggle for access to 'crude and material things without which no refined and spiritual things could exist' (Benjamin 1999: 246). What then is the working class 'in-itself' struggling for? 'In-itself' the working class struggles for better wages and conditions, and defends wage levels and conditions. It struggles against capital's 'were-wolf's hunger for surplus labour' and its destructive conquest for additional atoms of labour time, and thus against its reduction to a mere time's carcass. It struggles against a life constituting solely of labour-time and thus against a reduction of her human life to a mere economic resource. It struggles for respect, education, and recognition of human significance, and above all it struggles for food, shelter, clothing, warmth, love, affection, knowledge, and dignity. It struggles against the reduction of its life-time to labour-time, of its humanity to an economic resource, of its living existence to personified labour-time. Its struggle as a class 'in-itself' really is a struggle 'for-itself': for life, human distinction, life-time, and above all, satisfaction of basic human needs. It does all of this in conditions (*Zustände*) in which the increase in material wealth that it has produced, pushes beyond the limits of the capitalist form of wealth.Every so-called trickle-down effect that capitalist accumulation might bring forth presupposes a prior and sustained trickle up in the capitalist accumulation of wealth. And then society 'suddenly finds itself put back into a state of momentary barbarism; it appears as if famine, a universal war of devastation had cut off the supply of every means of subsistence' (Marx and Engels 1996: 18-19). For Benjamin and Marx, the experience of being cut off from the means of subsistence makes the oppressed class the depository of historical knowledge. It is the class struggle that 'supplies a unique experience with the past', and understanding of the present (Benjamin 1999: 254). Whether this experience 'turns concrete in the changing forms of repression as resistance to repression' (Adorno 1973: 265) or whether it turns concrete in forms of repression is a matter of experienced history. Critically understood, and in distinction to the classical tradition, historical materialism is not only a critique of things understood dogmatically. That is, at its best it thinks against the flow of history and, as such, it really 'brush[es] history against the grain' (Benjamin 1999: 248) so that the critical reason of human emancipation does not become 'a piece of the politics it was supposed to lead out of' (Adorno 1973: 143).

The existence of human labour as an economic factor of production does not entail reduction of consciousness to economic consciousness. It entails the concept of economy as an experienced concept, and economic consciousness as an experienced consciousness. At the very least, economic consciousness is an unhappy consciousness. It is this consciousness that demands reconciliation. In sum, 'freedom is a hollow delusion for as long as one class of humans can starve another with impunity. Equality is a hollow delusion for as long as the rich exercise the right to decide over the life and death of others' (Roux 1985: 147).

Postscript

Where is the positive? The society of human purposes can be defined in negation only. History holds no promise at all. History does nothing. It is made. In the struggle against a negative world nothing is certain, expect misery itself. Nevertheless, uncertainty is also an experienced concept of struggle (Bonefeld 2004). Historically, it has assumed the form of the 'council', the Commune, the Raete, the assemblies: this democracy of the street, which, despite appearance to the contrary, manifests no impasse at all. It is the laboratory of the society of free and equal—its validity is its own uncertainty.

NOTES

1. On the distinction between deplorable situations and deplorable conditions, see Bonefeld (2000).
2. Adapted from the German original that uses the phrase 'verrueckte' Form. In German verrueckt has a double meaning: man and displaced. I translate this as 'perverted'.
3. The social calamity of capitalist development is taken from Karl Marx (1983: 416).
4. On this see Schmidt (1983) and Bonefeld (2010a).
5. I use this phrase in reference to Holloway's (2010) negative theory of capitalism.
6. On the connection between St. Petersburg and Kronstadt, see Brendel (2002).
7. The notion of thinking out of history rather than about history, derives from Adorno's (1973) negative dialectics which argues that for thought to decipher capitalist society, it needs to think out of society. For him, thinking about society, or about history, amounts to an argument based on hypothetical judgements that treat the world as an 'as if', leaving reality itself untouched and leading to dogmatic claims about its character. Critical theory, at least this is its critical intent, deciphers society from within, seeking its dissolution as a continuum of inevitable and irresistible social forces, political events, economic laws (of scarcity), and empirical data. On this, see Bonefel (2012).

8. The 'rosary that slips through our hands' refers to Benjamin's critique of an historical materialism that has slipped into the theoretical method of historicism, which conceives of history as a sequence of events.

REFERENCES

Adorno, T.W. (1962), *Einleitungzur Musiksoziologie*, Suhrkamp, Frankfurt.

Adorno, T.W. (1969) 'MarginalienzuTheorie und Praxis', in *Stichworte Kritische Modelle 2*, Suhrkamp, Frankfurt.

Adorno, T.W. (1970), *Ästhetische Theorie*, Suhrkamp, Frankfurt.

Adorno, T.W. (1972), Soziologische Schriften I, in *Gesammelte Werke*, Vol. 8, Suhrkamp, Frankfurt.

Adorno, T.W. (1973), *Negative Dialectics*, Routledge, London.

Adorno, T.W. (1975), *Gesellschaftstheorie und Kulturkritik*, Suhrkamp, Frankfurt.

Adorno, T.W. (1978), *Minima Moralia: Reflections from Damaged Life*, Verso, London.

Adorno, T.W. (1993a), 'Einleitung', in *Der Positivismusstreit in der deutschen Soziologie*, dtv, Munich.

Adorno, T.W. (1993b), 'ZurLogik der Sozialwissenschaften', in *Der Positivismusstreit in der deutschen Soziologie*, dtv, Munich.

Adorno, T.W. (2008a), *Lectures on History and Freedom*, Polity, Cambridge.

Adorno, T.W. (2008b), *Lectures on Negative Dialectics*, Polity, Cambridge.

Adorno, T.W. and M. Horkheimer (2011), *Towards a New Manifesto*, Verso, London.

Backhaus, H.G. (1992), 'Between Philosophy and Science: Marxian Social Economy as Critical Theory', in Bonefeld, W.R. Gunn and K. Psychopedis (eds.) *Open Marxism*, Vol. I, Pluto, London.

Benjamin, W. (1999), *Illuminations*, Pimlico, London.

Bonefeld, W. (2000), 'Die Betroffenheit und die Vernunft der Kritik', in Bruhn, J., M. Dahlmann, and C. Nachmann (eds.) *Kritik der Politik*, Ca Ira, Freiburg.

Bonefeld, W. (2004), 'Uncertainty and Social Autonomy', *The Commoner*, No. 8, Winter 2004, pp. 1-6.

Bonefeld, W. (2010a), 'History and Human Emancipation', *Critique*, 38/1, pp. 61-73.

Bonefeld, W. (2010b), 'Abstract Labour: Against its Nature and on its Time', *Capital & Class*, Vol. 34/2, pp. 257-76.

Bonefeld, W. (2012), Negative Dialectics in Miserable Times: Notes on Adorno and Social Praxis', in *Journal of Classical Sociology* 12 (1), pp. 122-34.

Brendel, C. (2002), 'Kronstadt: Proletarian Spin-Off of the Russian Revolution', in Bonefeld, W. and S. Tischler (eds.) *What is to be Done?*, Ashgate, Aldershot.

Clarke, S. (1992), *Marx, Marginalism and Modern Sociology*, 2nd ed., Palgrave, London.

Gambino, F. (2003), 'A Critique of the Fordism of the Regulation School', in W. Bonefeld (ed.), *Revolutionary Writing*, Autonomedia, New York, 2003.

Holloway, J. (2010), *Crack Capitalism*, Pluto, London.

Horkheimer, M. (1985), *The Eclipse of Reason*, Continuum, New York.

Horkheimer, M. and T.W. Adorno (1972), *Dialectics of Enlightenment*, Verso, London.

Marcuse, H. (1958), *Soviet Marxism: A Critical Analysis*, Routledge & Kegan Paul, London.

Marcuse, H. (1964), *One Dimensional Man*, Routledge & Kegan Paul, London.

Marcuse, H. (1988), 'Philosophy and Critical Theory', in ibid. *Negations*, Free Association Press, London.

Marx, K. (1970), Critique of the Gotha Programme, in Marx/Engels *Selected Works*, Vol. 3, Progress Publishers, Moscow.

Marx, K. (1972), *Theorien des Mehrwerts*, MEW 26.3, Dietz, Berlin.

Marx, K. (1973), *Grundrisse*, Penguin, London.

Marx, K. (1975), Contribution to the Critique of Hegel's 'Philosophy of Right'. Introduction, in *Collected Works*, Vol. 3, Lawrence & Wishart, London.

Marx, K. (1966), *Capital*, Vol. III, Lawrence & Wishart, London.

Marx, K. (1979), *Das Kapital*, MEW 23, Dietz, Berlin.

Marx, K. (1980), *Die heilige Familie*, in MEW 2, Dietz, Berlin.

Marx, K. (1983), *Capital*, Vol. I, Lawrence & Wishart, London.

Marx, K. and F. Engels (1996), *The Communist Manifesto*, Pluto, London.

Marx, K. and F. Engels (1976), The German Ideology, in *Collected Works*, Vol. 5, International Publishers, New York.

Pinkus, T. (ed.) (1975), *Conversations with Lukacs*, MIT Press, Cambridge, MA.

Roux, J. (1985), 'Das "Manifest der Enragés"', in ibid, *Freiheitwird die Welt erobern*, Reden und Schriften, Röderberg, Frankfurt.

Schmidt, A. (1974), 'Praxis', in *Gesellschaft: Beiträgezur Marxschen Theorie 2*, Suhrkamp, Frankfurt.

Schmidt, A. (1983), *History and Structure*, MIT Press, Cambridge MA.

Tischler, S. (2005), 'Time of Reification and Time of Insubordination. Some Notes' in Bonefeld, W. and K. Psychopedis (eds.) *Human Dignity*, Ashgate, Aldershot.

4

On the Question of Alternatives

A TALK TO THE LONDON ANARCHIST BOOK FAIR, OCTOBER 2010

I

I want to start with a quotation from a Socialist Workers Party poster that I saw on the way to the Anarchist Book Fair. It said: 'Fight Back the Wrecking Tory Cuts'. There is no doubt that the cuts have to be rejected and will be opposed; society will try to protect itself from misery. 'Fight Back the Wrecking Tory Cuts' says something disarmingly obvious, and yet there is more to it than it seems. What does 'fight back the cuts' entail as a positive demand? It says no to cuts, and thus demands a capitalism not of cuts but of redistribution from capital to labour; it demands a capitalism that creates jobs not for capitalist profit but for gainful and purposeful employment, its premise is a capitalism that supports conditions not of exploitation but of well-being, and it projects a capitalism that offers fair wages ostensibly for a fair days work, grants equality of conditions, etc. What a wonderful capitalism that would be! One is reminded of Marx's judgment when dealing with the socialist demand for a state that renders capital profitable without ostensibly exploiting the workers: poor dogs they want to treat you as humans!

This idea of a capitalism without cuts, a benevolent capitalism in short, is of course as old as capitalism itself. In our time, this idea is connected with the so-called global financial capitalism that came to the fore in the 1970s. At that time, Bill

Warren, for example, argued that all that needed to be done was to change the balance of power, of class power, to achieve, as it were, a socialist hegemony within capitalism—a strangely comforting idea, which presupposes that the hegemony of capital within capitalism is contingent upon the balance of class forces and thus changeable—ostensibly in favour of a socialist capitalism achieved by socialist majorities in parliament making capitalism socialist through law and parliamentary decisions. What an easy thing socialism is! All one has to do is vote for the right party, shift the balance of forces in favour of socialism, and enact the right laws. With the left enjoying hegemony, the state becomes a means to govern over capital, or as Warren saw it, to make money work, not for profit but for jobs, for wages, for welfare. This argument makes it seem as if money only dissociated itself from productive engagement because of a certain change in the balance of class forces. And the crisis of accumulation that began in the late 1960s—what do we make of this?

In the 1980s Austin Mitchell demanded the same thing in his book *Market Socialism*. He says 'we need a state who will make money its servant, so that it is put to work for growth and jobs, rather than the selfish purposes of the merchants of greed.' Later this became a demand of the anti-globalisation movement, from economists such as Joseph Stiglitz to proponents of the Tobin Tax, from journalists such as Naomi Klein, who wanted no logo, to political economists such as Leo Panitch who wanted the state to de-commodify social relations by putting money to work on behalf of workers within protected national economies—protected from the world market.

In the last 20 years 'fighting back finance capitalism' was a rallying cry for those who declared to make money create jobs, conditions, employment, that is, to create—in other words—the capitalism of jobs, of employment, of conditions.

Within the critical Marxist tradition, this sort of position is associated with the social-democratic conception of the state. This conception focuses on the way in which social wealth is distributed. It has little to say about the production of that wealth, other than that the labourer should receive fair wages for a fair day's work. The perspective does not take into account the way in which we as a society organise our social reproduction; the question of the economic form of our exchange with nature is seen as a matter of benevolent state intervention.

This separation between production and distribution presupposes something that is not taken into account: distribution presupposes production. Distribution presupposes a well-functioning, growing economy, that is, capitalist accumulation. So the social-democratic position, which I outlined earlier with Panitch, Bill Warren and others, including the SWP, in fact translates working-class demands—for conditions, for wages, for security, in some cases for life—into the demand for rapid capitalist accumulation, as the economic basis for job creation.

Let's talk about the working class, this class of "hands' that does the work. Does the critique of class society entail an affirmative conception of class, which says that the working class deserves a better deal—employment, wages, condition. Is class really an affirmative category? Or is it a critical category of a false society—a class society in which wealth is produced by a 'class of hands' that have nothing but their labour-power to sell? To be a productive labourer is not a piece of luck, it is a great misfortune. The critique of class does not find its resolution in a better paid and better employed working class. It finds its resolution only in a classless society.

Class analysis is not some sort of flag-waving on behalf of the working class. Such analysis is premised on the perpetuation of the worker as a seller of labour power, which is the very condition of the existence of capitalist social relations. Affirmative conceptions of class, however well-meaning and benevolent in their intentions, presuppose the working class as a productive factor of production that deserves a better, a new deal.

As I stated right at the start, it is obviously the case that the more the working class gets the better. For it is the working class that produces the wealth of nations. It is the class that works. Yet; what is a fair wage?

In Volume three of *Capital* Marx says something like this:

'price of labour is just like a yellow logarithm'. Political economy in other words is indeed a very scholarly dispute about how the booty of labour may be divided, or distributed. Who gets what? Who bears the cuts? Who produces capitalist wealth, and what are the social presuppositions and consequences of the capitalist organisation of the social relations of production, an organisation that without fail accumulates great wealth for the class that hires workers to do the work.

II

I want to step back a bit to 1993, just after the deep recession of the early 1990s and the second of the two European currency crises. It was on December 24, 1993 that the *Financial Times* announced that globalisation—a term which hardly had any currency until then—is the best wealth-creating system ever invented by mankind. And it said, unfortunately two thirds of the world's population gained little or no substantial advantage from rapid economic growth.

In the developed world the lowest quarter of income earners had witnessed a trickle up rather than a trickle down. So since the mid-1970s, and Warren picks up on this, we have a system where money, the incarnation of wealth, is invested—incestuously as it were—into itself, opening a huge gap, a dissociation between an ever receding though in absolute terms growing productive base. This created something akin to an upside down pyramid where a great and ever increasing mortgage, an ever greater and ever increasing claim on future surplus value accumulated—mortgaging the future exploitation of labour. This mortgage tends to become fictitious at some point when investor confidence disappears—when, in other words, the exploitation of labour in the present does not keep up with the promise of future extraction of value.

It is against this background that Martin Wolf argued in 2001 'what is needed is honest and organised coercive force'. He said that in relationship to the developing world. And Martin Wolf is right—from his perspective. In order to guarantee debt, in order to guarantee money, coercion is the means to render austerity effective. Or as Soros said in 2003: 'Terrorism provided not only the ideal legitimisation but also the ideal enemy for the unfettered coercive protection of a debt-ridden free market society', because, he says, 'it is invisible and never disappears'.

So the premise of a politics of austerity is in fact the ongoing accumulation of humans on the pyramid of capitalist accumulation. Its blind eagerness for plunder requires organised coercive force in order to sustain this huge mortgage, this huge promise of future exploitation, here in the present.

Martin Wolf's demand for the strong state does not belie neoliberalism, which is wrongly caricatured as endorsing the weak and ineffectual state. Neoliberalism does not demand weakness from the state. 'Laissez faire', said the late Sir Alan Peacock, formerly a Professor of Economics, 'is no answer to riots'.

'Law', says Carl Schmitt, the legal philosopher of Nazism, 'does not apply to chaos.' For law to apply order must exist. Law presupposes order. Order is not the consequence of law. Law is effective only on the basis of order. And that is as Hayek put it in the Road to Serfdom: 'Laissez faire is a highly ambiguous and misleading description of the principles on which a liberal policy is based.' 'The neoliberal state', he says, 'is a planner too, it is a planner for competition'. Market freedom in other words, requires the market police, that is the state, for its protection and maintenance.

Capitalist social relations, Schmitt claims, are protected by an enlightened state, and in times of crisis a more or less authoritarian direction becomes unavoidable. Chaos and disorder create the state of emergency which call for the establishment of a strong, market facilitating, order making state. The state is the political form of the force of law—of law making violence.

For the neoliberals, disorder has nothing to do with markets. It is to do with what they perceive as irrational social action. That is, they see the democratisation or politicisation of social labour relations as a means of disorder, it undermines markets and renders the state ungovernable. The state however, argue the neoliberal authors, has to govern to maintain order, and with it, the rule of law, the relations of exchange, the law of contract. Free markets function on the basis of order; and order, they argue, entails an ordered society; and an ordered society is not a society that is politicised, but one which is in fact governed—by the democracy of demand and supply, which only the strong state is able to facilitate, maintain, and protect.

III

What is the alternative?

I think the difficulty of conceiving of human self-emancipation has to do with the very idea of human emancipation. This idea is distinct from the pursuit of profit, the seizure of the state, the pursuit and preservation of political power, economic value and economic resources. It follows a completely different idea of human development—and it is this, which makes it so very difficult to conceive, especially in a time of 'cuts'. One cannot think, it seems, about anything else but 'cuts, cuts, cuts'. Our language, which a few years ago spoke of the Paris Commune, the Zapatistas, Council Communism, and the project of self-emancipation that these terms summoned, has been replaced by the language of cuts, and fight back, and bonuses, and unfairness, etc.. And then suddenly, imperceptibly it seems, this idea of human emancipation—in opposition to a life compelled to be lived for the benefit of somebody's profit, a life akin to an economic resource—gives way to the very reality that it seeks to change and from which it cannot get away—a reality of government cuts and of opposition against cuts. Government governs those who oppose it. Human emancipation is however not a derivative of capitalist society—it is its alternative, yet, as such an alternative it is premised on what it seeks to transcend. The SWP poster, with which I started, focuses this premise as an all-embracing reality—cuts or no cuts, that is the question.

What is the alternative? Let us ask the question of capitalism differently, not as a question of cuts but as a question of labour-time. How much labour-time was needed in 2010 to produce the same amount of commodities as was produced in 1990? Fifty per cent? Thirty per cent? Twenty per cent? Whatever the percentage might be, what is certain is that labour-time has not decreased. It has increased. What is certain, too, is that despite this increase in wealth, the dependent masses are subjected to a politics of austerity as if famine, a universal war of devastation had cut off the supply of every means of subsistence. What a calamity: In the midst of 'austerity', this rational means to perpetuate an irrational mode of production, in which the reduction of the hours of labour needed for the production of the means of subsistence appears in reality as a crisis of finance, money and cash, the struggle over the appropriation of additional atoms of labour-time pursues as if the reduction of the life-time of the worker to labour-time is the resolution to the crisis of debt, finance, and cash flow. Indeed it is. Time is money. And if time really is money, than Man is nothing—except a time's carcass.

And here, in this calamity, there is hope. The hope is that the struggle against cuts, is also a struggle for something.

What does the fight against cuts entail? It is a struggle against the reduction of life-time to labour-time. The fight against cuts is in fact a fight for a life. For the dependent masses, wages and welfare benefits are the means with which to obtain the means of subsistence. The fight against the cuts is a fight for the provision of the means of subsistence. And that is, it is a conflict between antagonistic interests, one determining that time is money, the other demanding the means of subsistence. This demand, as I argued at the start, might well express itself uncritically as a demand for a politics of jobs and wages, affirming the need for rapid accumulation as the means of job-creation. It might not. It might in fact politicise the social labour relations, leading to the question why the development of the productive forces at the disposal of society have become too powerful for this society, bringing financial disorder and requiring austerity to maintain it. Such politicisation, if indeed it is to come about, might well express, in its own words, Jacques Roux's dictum that

> freedom is a hollow delusion for as long as one class of humans can starve another with impunity. Equality is a hollow delusion for as long as the rich exercise the right to decide over the life and death of others.